# YOUR ROOTS
# DON'T
# DEFINE YOU

# YOUR ROOTS DON'T DEFINE YOU

### Transform Your Life.
### Create Your Comeback.

## CHRIS APPLETON

HANOVER
SQUARE
PRESS

**HANOVER
SQUARE
PRESS™**

Recycling programs
for this product may
not exist in your area.

ISBN-13: 978-1-335-00142-9

Your Roots Don't Define You: Transform Your Life. Create Your Comeback.

Hanover Square Press
22 Adelaide St. West, 41st Floor
Toronto, Ontario M5H 4E3, Canada
HanoverSqPress.com

HarperCollins Publishers
Macken House, 39/40 Mayor Street Upper,
Dublin 1, D01 C9W8, Ireland
www.HarperCollins.com

Printed in U.S.A.

To Billy and Kitty-Blu,
the loves of my life.

# CONTENTS

# FOREWORD

## by Kris Jenner

One thing I've learned in this life is that beauty is never just about what's on the outside. It's about strength, perseverance, grace under pressure—and knowing exactly who you are, even when the world, and your roots, try to tell you otherwise.

That's what drew me to Chris Appleton from the very beginning. Yes, the hair was iconic—the slicked-back ponytails, the flawless waves, the jaw-dropping red-carpet transformations. His work didn't just follow trends; it set them. But what captivated me most wasn't just what Chris could do—it was who he *is*. His heart. His journey. And the way he uses his gift not just to style hair, but to lift spirits and transform lives.

This book, this movement of your roots not defining you, isn't just about makeovers. It's about the moments behind the mirror: the self-doubt, the struggle, the healing, the breakthrough that happens when you decide to own your truth.

I've had the joy of sitting in Chris's chair and calling him a friend. And let me tell you—when Chris does your hair, it's not just an appointment. It's an experience.

It's laughter. It's truth. It's realignment. And yes, it's *a lot* of glam. But more than anything, it's about rediscovering who you are—and walking out feeling lighter, freer, and more *yourself*.

In this book, Chris gives that experience to *you*.

*Your Roots Don't Define You* isn't just about changing how you look—it's about reclaiming who you are. It's about letting go of the weight of your past and stepping into the power of your story.

Chris knows what it feels like to not fit the mold. To be judged before you've had a chance to speak. And yet here he is, sharing his truth with courage, vulnerability, and that signature Chris Appleton sparkle.

That's what makes this book so powerful. It's not fluff. It's not surface. It's real. It's raw.

As a mother, a manager, and a woman who's reinvented herself more than once, I know how important it is to have people in your life who *see* you—and help you become the version of yourself you always dreamed of being, before the world told you otherwise.

Chris is that person for so many. And now, through this book, he gets to be that person for you.

This is your mirror. Your moment. Your comeback. Not the kind that fades when the lights go out—but the kind that *lasts*, because it's built from within.

Chris hands you the tools, the stories, and the truth to help you rewrite your narrative—and step boldly, beautifully, un-apologetically into your future.

Whether you picked up this book for the beauty, for the change, or simply to be reminded you're not alone—you're in the right place. Where you came from doesn't define you. If I had let my past define me, I wouldn't be where I am today.

Chris has lived through the hard parts—and turned them into something beautiful. He reminds us that the most powerful transformations come not from perfection, but from *authenticity*.

So here's to letting go of what holds us back.

Here's to honoring where we came from—but refusing to be limited by it. And here's to my dear friend Chris, for remind-ing us that real beauty begins when we finally believe *we* get to define who we are.

Now turn the page. Your transformation is waiting.

# INTRODUCTION

You know that feeling.

The one right after a fresh haircut or blowout when you catch yourself in a reflection and think, *Okay! I see you!* Like you could walk into an interview, a party, a date, even an awkward run-in with your ex and absolutely own it.

Well, I specialize in creating that feeling.

I've been doing hair since I was thirteen, back when my first "clients" were my mum and the models in magazines I'd draw different hairstyles on. Since then, I've seen firsthand how something as simple as a haircut can spark real, powerful change. Not just on the outside but deep within, where it matters most.

I've seen women find the strength to start over after heartbreak, career catastrophes, loss, burnout, or those seasons of just waking up one day wondering, *Is this really it?* And believe me, I've been there, too. I've failed far more than I've succeeded. I've dealt with crippling insecurities and lived the mess, the doubt, and the reinvention. So, if you're standing at any kind of crossroads in your life right now, please know that I see you, I feel you, I am you.

You are not alone.

It's never too late to transform, to reinvent, and to create a comeback that no one saw coming. And if you've ever questioned that, I'm here to prove otherwise.

You're probably wondering, *Why should I listen to you? You just do hair.* Well, yeah, I do hair, but what I do is so much more than that. I listen. I watch. I get you and get IT.

On the outside, many might describe my job as just to make people look great. But to me, the far more important part is making them *feel* great. I have worked with and am trusted by some of the most confident, enviable, and gorgeous women on the planet. Nothing is impossible in my world, and I have a knack for guiding women to step into their best selves.

The relationship between a hairdresser and a client is one of the most profound bonds you'll ever have. It's akin to the therapist's couch in many ways. Clients come to me during pivotal moments—before a big event, when they're experiencing significant change, after a breakup, or when they need a fresh start. These are the moments when people let their guard down. Your hairdresser is probably one of the few people you feel comfortable enough with to be completely honest and vulnerable, to confront fears and to embrace change. Memories are attached to hair; people open up and let go when they feel safe. A great hairdresser doesn't just listen, they mine for a deeper understanding. They see the version of you that you're trying to bring to life.

This is a connection I build that goes beyond the physical act of cutting, coloring, and styling hair. A hairdresser is not merely a service provider; they are a confidant, a collaborator, a therapist, and cheerleader. It's a relationship built through every appointment, conversation, every moment of trust. Some people don't get this level of intimacy and compassion from even their closest relationships.

I don't see the same limitations that people set for themselves. I see *through* them. I help them lift them away, one by one, until we reach the core of who they are. I'm not just altering appearance; I'm touching your identity, shaping how you see yourself and want to be seen.

Sitting in a hairdresser's chair is a microcosm of life's broader journey. It is a moment of vulnerability, introspection, and power. Change is not only essential for growth; it is inevitable.

One of the biggest things I hear from my clients is that, on both a literal and figurative level, their roots not only box them into a set of limits, but they define who they are (ugly duckling, incapable, unlucky, damaged beyond repair, etc.—and trust me, I've been called all of these more than once). We all wrestle with our own inner voices telling us we can't do something.

I know what it's like to be insecure about social interactions—wondering if I said the wrong thing, feeling dependent on external validation from my friends or social media, and to struggle with self-worth when I go down the rabbit hole of comparison. Rejection and embarrassment were my constant companions, and I've battled crippling anxiety and insecurities—which still pop up from time to time—for much longer than I've felt confidence and peace. I've been through the fire and come out the other side successful because I became who I was meant to be.

If you're chasing a dream while people tell you it's impossible, or struggling to believe you deserve what you want, I see you. If you're stuck in a cycle of self-doubt, overthinking, procrastination, or insecurity, I know you. If you feel trapped by the pain and shame of your past, your limiting beliefs, or the expectations placed on you, I've been right where you are.

I have worked with the world's most famous women, and guess what? They've all had the same debilitating fears and anxieties that you and I feel. Our circumstances and stories may be different, but the feelings are universal. The constant pressure to perform or be at the top of our game, but also be riddled with imposter syndrome and a crisis of self-worth. The thin line you have to walk of having ambition and wanting things but not seeming self-serving or greedy. The desire to fit in, but also the necessity of having to stand out. The feeling of never being enough in a thousand different ways.

We all carry the weight of these feelings. Even those who walk the red carpet or show up on your socials and seem to be living a perfect life, with the perfect hair, the perfect body, the perfect boyfriend, poolside with a frozen margarita in one hand and the *Read with Jenna*'s book club pick in the other.

But what if you had the chance to reinvent yourself from the ground up? Not just by changing your hairstyle or your hair color, but by transforming your entire approach to self-care and the self-image that was programmed at a time when you were too vulnerable to challenge and investigate it?

What if the shame, failures, and pain of your past could fuel a comeback that no one expected—and you could use your roots to no longer limit you but give you an invaluable blueprint to become the person you were destined to be?—from the inside out.

Your roots, whether they be the ones I color or the place that you came from, no longer have the power to persuade you into thinking that "this is it" for you. I have made a business out of lifting the limitations my clients have imposed on themselves.

I don't have all the answers, but I've learned so much from doing what I do. And what I know for sure is this: if you let your roots define you—whether the literal ones we color in our hair or the ones tied to our past—you'll never know who the real you is. You'll spend your whole life as an "image manager," shapeshifting, pretending to be what everyone else thinks you should be.

If you're reading this page right now, you already have the fight in you.

In this book, I'm giving you the same thing I give to every woman I style: an opportunity to release your past, rebrand yourself, and walk into your future with unapologetic confidence and style. It's a call to action for anyone who's ever felt trapped by their background, self-perception, or even their hair.

Shall we get into it, then?

PART I

## WHO YOU ARE NOW

# 1.

# You Don't Have to Lie in the Bed You Made Forever

## *Your New Life Is Waiting*

I know about transformation. The real kind. The deep, internal, life-altering kind. I know how hard it is. I know how long it takes. I know you can probably come up with every reason and excuse not to want it.

Everyone has the power to transform their lives, but most people don't. Why? Because it's fucking hard. Because staying the same is easier. Finding an excuse for why you can't change is much easier than committing to it and following through. Making excuses is more comfortable than taking action. Most people make their bed and then lie in it forever, even if it's uncomfortable or they've outgrown it.

Change also isn't neat. No matter how much you try, it isn't clean, simple, or something you can plan for. It's messy. It's terrifying. It's raw. It's standing at the edge of everything you know and being brave enough to take a step into something uncertain. It's challenging the limits of what you're capable of and what's possible.

I can practically see you shrugging right now because you've heard this before. Volumes have been written about change. Every fourth book at the store or video on your feed is about change. It's everywhere. But talking isn't doing.

For a long time, I thought change was something you controlled. Something you could execute in measured steps—like how I can methodically take jet-black hair to platinum blonde—or that you could plan it through minor adjustments—like curbing my habit of interrupting when I'm excited or trying to be agreeable to avoid conflict. I thought that gradually, you could shape yourself into who you wanted to be.

But real change, the kind that shifts your entire existence (yes, I'm going there), doesn't work that way. It happens in moments you don't expect. It happens when life forces you to face the truth you've been running from.

Change has to start somewhere. Sometimes it's packing a bag and walking out the door. Other times, it's finally speaking a truth you've tried to avoid and deny for too long. And sometimes, it's something small—so small, it almost feels trivial. And sometimes, you realize it was never about the thing itself. It was about what it *represented*. About choosing yourself; parting with the dead ends in life.

Just like cutting your hair.

People scoff at the idea that a haircut can change your life. *It's just hair,* they say. *It'll grow back like nothing happened.* But if you've ever watched pieces of yourself fall to the floor, suspended in the space between who you were when you walked into the salon and who you're becoming, the change transpiring before your eyes—you know the real truth. In the sacred space of the salon chair is a world of possibility that doesn't exist elsewhere, not because it can't, but because you don't indulge yourself in your unfiltered aspirations outside of the safety of this cocoon.

There's a moment after the scissors do their work when a person looks at their reflection and sees a version of themselves they haven't seen before. Or maybe they have seen it—years ago, before life started piling layers on top. In that flicker of recognition, that's the shift.

## IT'S ABOUT PERMISSION

I had a client once, a woman in her forties, who was quiet when she first came into the salon. She sat down in my chair and I could see right away her energy was loaded with intensity. I ran my fingers through her long, dark waist-length hair, assessing it. It was immaculate. Not a split end to be found. I could tell from the condition of her hair that she did all the right things: used quality hair products, avoided heat damage, and probably slept on a satin pillowcase with her hair in a long braid to protect it. Yet the hair was so long that it was all you saw when you looked at her.

"What are we doing today?" I asked, assuming that I was about to do a trim.

"I've been thinking lately . . . If I cut it all off, can you donate it somewhere to make a wig?" She met my eyes in the mirror, and I could see that there was something deeper happening.

"Your hair is in beautiful condition," I told her, "and I can absolutely get it to the right people. But you don't have to cut it all off. I could take off ten inches to donate, and you'd still have hair to your shoulder blades."

She let out the kind of contemptuous chuckle that has history to it. The kind that says *I've been down this road before.*

"If I had a dollar for every time I've chickened out of committing to real change . . ." She swallowed hard. "I'd have fifteen years of dollars."

When someone comes to me asking for a drastic change, I always want to spend the time up front to really talk with them and make sure it's not an impulsive decision that will lead to regret.

She asked me to chop her waist-length hair into a blunt bob.

"Nobody *sees* me anymore. Not even my husband. Not even me, really."

She went on to share how she felt invisible and overlooked.

None of the little changes she had made over the years ever lasted. She had decided it was time to be bold and to be seen. I agreed.

When I made the first big cut, taking off fourteen inches, she exhaled long and slow, like she was releasing something long and heavy she'd been holding for years.

"You okay?" I was afraid she might suddenly be getting second thoughts.

"No. I found out this week that I didn't get the promotion that I should have gotten. And when my boss told me I wasn't getting it because I was too valuable to him where I was, I *thanked* him. Can you believe that? I thanked him for not giving me the job I wanted and deserved."

I understood her frustration. I've seen so many people who find themselves at a place in their life where they are taken for granted or undervalued. She told me that she felt stuck in the same version of herself that had stopped evolving, but she had been too afraid to let go. She had made her bed a long time ago—and now it felt too small.

She needed to do something to shake things up or she felt like she would explode.

"If I don't push myself and demand more," she said, "I'm never going to get what I want."

She urged me to go even shorter and after I was done cutting her long mane into a sleek sophisticated bob, she studied herself in the mirror, tilted her head, and said, "I should've done this a decade ago."

This new hairstyle felt like a gateway change. She left the salon feeling liberated, not just because of the cut—but because she finally did something. She took an action that shifted her mindset. She could see new possibilities for herself and a path forward.

The haircut was never about the hair. It's about permission. It's about proving to yourself that you are not stuck. That you can evolve. That the person you see in the mirror is allowed to not look the same forever.

People talk about reinvention like it's some grand, sweeping event. Like you have to move to a new city, get a new job, and become a completely different person. But real reinvention? It happens in the small moments, with each snip of the scissors. The tiny, deliberate choices that resonate inside you, affirming that you're ready for something new, one bit at a time. And that doesn't always come with a clean "before" and "after."

I'm a hairdresser, so of course, I will tell you that changing your hair is the easiest way to start changing your life. External change is often the precursor to a more significant change. It won't fix everything. It won't heal wounds, undo mistakes, or erase grief. But it might be the first domino to fall. The first spark of a fire you've been afraid to light.

When you look different, naturally, you feel different. When you feel different, you act differently. You stand taller and take up more space. You find a well of confidence and courage that wasn't there before.

You feel emboldened to be assertive, take risks, and go for what you want. You see yourself as someone capable of change because you've already started. You're excited to be you.

Why not chase that feeling every day? Why not grab hold of your one precious life with both hands and shape it into something extraordinary? Isn't the goal to be your best, brightest, happiest, and most fulfilled self?

## OBEY THE PHYSICS

*It's not that easy*, you think. I thought this, too. But guess what? It can be that easy. I know that staying stuck is just easier in the short term. But the consequences are devastating in the long term. Ask me how I know.

People cling to what's familiar, even when it's making them miserable. They stay in bad relationships, tolerate jobs they despise, live with hair they don't know what to do with. I'm begging you to ask yourself: For *what*? To prove you can? To have a false sense of safety and security? Who wins in this situation?

Your inertia keeps you doing nothing, remaining unchanged. It's like Newton's first law of motion—an object at rest stays at rest unless acted upon by an external force. So be that force for yourself! Don't wait for someone else to slam you out of your unsatisfying life.

Inertia is inaction—the true silent enemy. It draws you into her warm delusional embrace and tells you that things are fine the way they are. That change is too hard, so why bother?

Inertia pats the cushion next to her on the bed you made forever ago, and tells you to settle in and watch as life goes on being lived by others, while you sit motionless, glued to a screen. Inertia keeps you rotting in that bed, forgetting that you don't even like it, that it isn't comfortable anymore.

I listened to the whispers of inertia for a long time. Let it keep me small. Let it convince me that staying put was safer than risking the unknown. Inertia capitalized on my fears and stoked my apprehensions, until the voice that wanted more out of my life got so loud that I could no longer stay still.

## GO MATTRESS SHOPPING

Again, not every transformation starts with a grand gesture. Sometimes, it's just getting out of that bed. Aren't you curious about what's waiting for you? Don't you want to know what's behind the door, over the wall, through the self-imposed ceiling (or whatever domestic metaphor speaks to you)? I did, and I think you do, too.

Your highest self is waiting for you to push it into existence.

It's not born out of apathy, it's not sitting dormant, and it's not atrophying from neglect.

When you get knocked down, you don't have to stay there. You don't have to lie in the bed you made forever. For one, you can make some simple improvements and upgrade it.

Maybe it can start small—wash your sheets, buy some colored pillows and shake up the scene.

Or here's a mind-blowing idea: go out and find a new bed! You wouldn't stay in a twin-size bed for the rest of your life just because you slept in one in your college dorm.

You're also allowed to go sleep somewhere else for a while. (Preferably, in the bed of someone hot.) When it comes to changing who you are, you can try out multiple beds, try out different selves and friend groups and styles until you find the one that feels right for you. Go mattress shopping. Sleep around as much as you want. In fact, I encourage it.

Doesn't this sound more enticing than rotting in old sheets until it becomes your deathbed?

The metaphor can go even further. In its tangible form, the quality and presentation of your bed speak to how you view and treat yourself. The bed is where you soothe and restore. It's where you invite others into your life. Your bed should be one of your favorite—if not your very favorite—places to be. If it isn't, then you're doing it wrong. You deserve a cloud to crawl into at the end of day.

So ask yourself, what is the right bed for you and the life of your making? Are you really happy with the one you have? Or will you look back years from now and think, *I wasted my twenties away on my job that didn't appreciate me* or *My thirties were sucked up by a toxic relationship that gaslit me into questioning myself.* You are the maker of your bed and the architect of your life. You can change the blueprint to match your evolution and ambitions.

When I'm with a client or a friend and they complain about not liking this or hating that—whether it's about how they look, their job, their boyfriend, or whatever—I always ask, "So what's your plan? What are you doing to change it?"

There's usually an awkward silence that follows.

It's always more fun to complain than to act. It's just human nature: People don't want to be accountable for changing their lives; they want something to happen that magically solves their problems. They want to wait for some outside projectile to come along and force them out of cruise control. But life has never worked that way. Change requires action.

There are no prizes for staying unhappy for the longest. There is no trophy for enduring misery. Awards are not bestowed on those who wait the longest for a bad situation to be over. Life doesn't reward you for not doing anything about your discontent. If you want something different, you have to go after it.

*Don't confuse "sticking it out" for just being stuck.*

It's up to you to create your opportunities where and when you can, even when they feel insignificant. You can reinvent yourself entirely and make a comeback that no one saw coming. And it can all start with something small.

So, what does the new you look like? Name it. Go deep. Get specific. Everyone wants better, but what is "better" for you? How do you want to be seen by others? What do you want to project? What are you trying to call in?

And what is in your way—besides yourself? What are the

literal obstacles, and how can you remove, overcome, or get around them?

Figure it out, make a plan, organize your thoughts, keep a journal, or write it in your notes app—whatever works for you and where you can measure and celebrate your progress. And why not start with a haircut! Sometimes, the slightest change is the spark that sets everything else in motion. If transformation is coming, why not make it look hot?

# 2.

# It's Called a Reflection for a Reason

## *There's More to Your Mirror than Meets the Eye*

Unsurprisingly, I spend an inordinate amount of time in front of a mirror. Not just looking at myself (though, let's be honest, I do plenty of that), but because mirrors are essential to my work. Over time, I've had to train myself to see past my reflection and focus on my real purpose instead of my face.

Even so, my relationship with mirrors? It's still complicated. I'm sure you can relate. Best friend, worst enemy, habit I can't quit, or all of the above? Check. Check. Check. Double-check.

Mirrors are EVERYWHERE. Mirrors have become ubiquitous and unavoidable. Your phone is a mirror. Your laptop screen is a mirror (plus that corner square on our Zoom calls, which, let's be honest, is really where we're all staring during a meeting). Every house and car window you walk past? Mirrors. You are constantly confronted with your image, and you can't help but look at yourself in every single one. The urge is almost irresistible, but mirrors are not always your friend.

You look at yourself every day and, nine times out of ten, you see exactly what you expect. But the face looking back at you isn't always the truth. Your perception warps your reflection, making it harder to see yourself accurately.

A big chunk of my own mirror time is also spent behind my client's chair, watching *them* confront *their* reflections. I can almost see the scrutiny running through their head: *Does my nose look weird? Have my eyes always been this asymmetrical? Why do I look so puffy? How did I not notice my eyebrows need shaping?*

Sitting in a hairstylist's chair and looking into a mirror is one of the few places you can be entirely honest with yourself. There's a rawness to it. You're naked, fully exposed to your scrutiny.

In my experience, the first voice you hear is the harshest critic. Rarely do my clients—even the most high-profile or highly stylized celebrities—sit down and instantly say, *"I look good."* I see them zero in on their flaws with laser focus. List all the things they dislike and the regrets of whatever damage they feel has been done.

Over time, the chair becomes a spontaneous confession booth, like I am a priest who will prescribe seven Hail Marys, deep condition twice a week, and only use heat tools for special occasions. Which, sometimes I do prescribe, because why not?

Mirrors don't lie, but don't tell the whole truth or the full story. They capture every detail in ruthless high definition, but fail to reflect your energy, essence, and the things that make you who you are. We're holistic beings in ways that mirrors can never capture. It's wild how something can be both brutally honest and deceptively incomplete.

Nowhere is this paradox more evident than when a client sits in my chair whose literal profession is being beautiful.

I've worked with one client in particular for years. She's an actress and a model, and when I say she is drop-dead gorgeous, I mean she is genetically blessed in a way few are in this lifetime. She's in demand, her star is ascendant by every measure, she has a very enviable boyfriend, and she seemingly has the kind of life people dream about.

By all appearances, she has few problems, other than finding enough time in her schedule for all the brand and modeling opportunities coming her way. And yet even she battles crippling insecurities. Without fail, every time we work together, she comes through my door like she's walking to the electric chair, not the styling chair. Her posture hangs, she avoids eye contact, and then sheepishly curls up in the chair, hiding her face in her hands.

The most recent time we worked together, her first words were, "Don't look at me. I'm atrocious."

"What are you saying? You've never looked atrocious a day in your life."

"I've been eating like shit. My skin is breaking out like crazy from all the makeup tests I had to do for my next movie, and my hair is fried."

"All temporary things that can be managed," I assured her.

"I was at a fitting earlier, and the mirror was so unflattering. It was one of those ones that makes you look slightly compressed and thick. You know what I mean? Like sometimes you get a long and skinny mirror that makes you look great, but sometimes you get a shitty mirror that makes you feel terrible about yourself? I hate mirrors. I wish I didn't have to see myself all the time."

"I know exactly what you're talking about. Getting a bad mirror can mess with you. It heightens all of your self-critical inclinations. But even good mirrors can warp our perceptions when you're focusing on the wrong thing," I suggest. "All you're seeing is the negative."

After all, mirrors are not the problem: our relationship with them is.

Feelings don't give a shit about facts. The only version of herself that she believes to be beautiful is the one that is glammed, lit, photographed, and edited by a fleet of professionals. This is such a common issue with celebrities or people who live in the spotlight: the duality of the glamorously beautiful swan public persona and the private "real life" where they feel like the everyday person. The woman she sees in the mirror on this random Wednesday does not hold the same worth, even though she's the same person. She doesn't think this version counts.

It's mad, completely mental . . . but entirely understandable. Insecurity finds everyone and spares no one. No exceptions. It doesn't matter how gorgeous, talented, or successful you are. No one is immune. When one version of you is idolized—whether it's you idolizing your future potential or others idolizing what you present to the world—it's impossible not to find yourself lacking whenever that self feels out of reach.

That is the bigger issue—more significant than people realize. You are so anxious to see something you don't like (or finding ways to fix it) that you've lost your ability to reflect on what's *behind* it and whether it's even true in the first place. And I don't mean "reflect" as in, look at your face, I mean literal self-reflection.

Everything moves too fast in our lives. We know our attention spans are shit, and no one needs yet another person to tell them that. We swipe and scroll, consuming things at lightning speed, barely registering anything before we've moved on.

Needless to say, true reflection is a fundamental necessity for personal development and growth.

Full stop. I cannot stress that enough.

Reflection has helped me identify my strengths and weaknesses, acknowledge my progress, and recognize what I truly want. Not just from my career, but from myself. It's more than glancing in the mirror to check the outer image; it's about daring to pause and look inward, beyond the hair, the glamour, and the accolades. When I take a step back, I can identify the patterns I keep repeating; the habits that hold me back. And I can start to unpack the limiting beliefs I've carried, often unknowingly, for years.

It's an uncomfortable but liberating process. Because when you're doing it the right way, self-reflection doesn't show you what you want, but what you *need*.

I remember one particular moment when this hit me hard. It wasn't backstage at a major fashion show or during a red-carpet walk. It was in a quiet, ordinary moment that completely shifted my perspective and changed my life. At that moment, on a random Tuesday, the reflection staring back at me wasn't just about my look, but about what I had survived, overcome—and who I was becoming *as a result*.

Sadly, people are more comfortable with avoidance than reflection. Some clients don't even meet their own eyes in the mirror throughout an entire haircut. They're glued to their phone, completely checked out from the experience, disconnected from themselves and only interested in seeing a result that makes them feel good.

I get it. If given a choice between the two, avoidance is undoubtedly easier. Looking away from the mirror is easy, but reflection takes grit and compassion. It takes a willingness to sit with the discomfort of seeing yourself—your actions and emotions, the history of anger problems behind your frown lines; your habit of working too much from your eye bags, the debt you've accrued from online shopping to soothe yourself, the dental issues from the unspoken things you hold in your clenched jaw and nightly teeth grinding. The things you need to change.

Reflection allows you to press Pause, reevaluate your experiences, and gain valuable insights into things that affect your relationships with your partners, family, friends, and associates.

Your face in the mirror is colored with shades and tones of your past and what you've been told about who you are: *You have your mother's eyes, your father's emotional avoidance, curls like Grandpa, and a strong singing voice like your aunt.* It tells you where you come from, or maybe what you'll grow into one day—like the receding hairline that runs in your family, which you worry will one day catch up to you and box you in.

But honest reflection, emotional and cerebral, can tell you who you are *now*.

Reflecting on your roots provides a framework for understanding what made you who you are, and it holds the answers to the questions you may not even know to ask. For years, I believed stories about myself that I couldn't even remember the source of. Stories I'd absorbed without questioning them. That I was the quiet, shy one, that I wasn't smart or couldn't learn, that my trajectory was limited by my differences.

Who told me I was this way? Why did I accept that version of myself? And why, as a grown man, did I still think things about myself that ring entirely false?

Why did I think the weight of my history, and even the heredity characteristics I was saddled with were all immutable whenever I looked in a mirror?

Examining the parts of yourself and your life that you need to change or let go of is neither comfortable nor fun. No one likes to illuminate the things they're still dragging behind them from the past or excavate old wounds, regrets, and insecurities.

But you know what else isn't fun? Looking in a mirror to see yourself through the same eyes, feeling that same sense of dread every time for the rest of your life—all because you can't find the tools to do something about it. And our biggest tools are confronting, considering, and reflecting. It's painful to confront the worst of our past, our inner voices and insecurities—but it's *more painful* to stay the same, letting the critics and baggage in your life win, because they won't let you go anywhere. What's the bigger cost?

You and I both are messy, imperfect, and utterly flawed human beings who fail and fuck up. But here's the truth: Who you are today is not confined by who you were yesterday. Who you are tomorrow is still unwritten. It's up for grabs. You get to decide.

So, what do you see when you look beyond your reflection and reflect?

Inner critics always speak the loudest, especially the ones in the mirror. We can't snap our fingers and make them go away, but sometimes it helps to just remember that's what they are— and they have a power to warp the truth.

So, can you turn down the volume? Instead of avoiding your gaze, how can you offer yourself the same grace, support, kindness, and empathy you would extend to a friend? How do you approach self-reflection with honesty, openness, and a nonjudgmental mindset?

## OVERRIDE THE HATERS INSIDE

Now that we've acknowledged the messy relationship between mirrors and inner critics, I want to share something I've shared with my clients. Something that works for me. It involves silencing the nasty voice that loves to chime in the second you look in the mirror. It's the voice that knows how to cut the deepest because it knows all of your secrets, worst fears, and insecurities. The hater inside you knows how to hurt you in ways no one else can come close to.

I think of my inner critic as my own Personal Hater. I imagine the source to be someone genuinely awful, like your middle school bully, or your least favorite person in the world. Someone with ZERO credibility, who is the last person on earth you would ever trust or even want to be around.

The sound of their voice is torturous to your ears. Just thinking of them makes you roll your eyes and think, *Shut the fuck up.* My Personal Hater sounds like someone from my past who constantly taunted me about every little thing, from how I looked to what I wanted to be. Last I heard, he ended up in a career of waste management that he hated. So, safe to say, we live different lives. His opinion is literal crap as far as I'm concerned.

Now, stand in front of a mirror and look at yourself. Notice every freckle, wrinkle, dimple, and detail of your face or whole body if it's full length. Name three things you genuinely appreciate about what you see. For example:

- The arch of my eyebrows is fierce.
- Stunning flecks of gold and green sparkle in my eyes.
- The natural wave of my hair looks effortlessly beachy today.

You are training yourself to look for positive proof first. Now, name three things your Personal Hater whispers in your ear. Examples:

- You look tired and puffy.
- Your nose is too big for your face.
- Your lips are too thin.

See? I told you he was a real wanker. Now, take a moment to reflect. Go a step beyond the surface level to consider what's behind the daggers. Where did these thoughts even come from?

Personal Haters don't appear out of nowhere. They're built from old comments and cultural noise. Let's trace them and their wanker opinions back to where they originated.

- **Source:** My mom always tells me I look tired and worries my eye bags will be permanent.
- **Source:** That kid in middle school made fun of my nose.
- **Source:** Every celebrity and fashion model has naturally full lips or lip filler.

Now let's take that reflection and look at ourselves in the mirror again, this time fact-checking your Personal Hater.

- **Fact:** I work and play hard. I *earned* these dark circles. The puffiness or fullness of my face changes with hormones, diet, age, and experiences. So fucking what.
- **Fact:** I have my father's nose. It connects me to my heritage, and I might miss that if I changed it. Some of the coolest and most talented people have a strong nose presence. They haven't been hindered by their noses, in fact their nose makes them even cooler. And I can always learn to contour if I want to alter how the proportions look.
- **Fact:** My lips suit my face. And lots of gorgeous celebrities *also* have thin lips. I can change it if I want. Refer to above. Do I need to? No.

Your Personal Hater is an unimaginative bully exploiting your weakest spots. The more you let your bully go unchecked, the worse they become. The telling thing is that when you trace your Personal Hater's words or opinions back, it's almost always echoes of the past informing the present.

Your Personal Hater isn't seeing you in the mirror—it's just replaying old, warped loops that are ready to be tossed.

When the voice of your Personal Hater pops up, CANCEL IT. SHUT IT DOWN. DO A SYSTEM OVERRIDE. Fact-check it immediately. Remind yourself what you *are* looking for. The good, the real, the truth. You are writing new computer code for your brain to look for positive proof that will silence your Personal Hater.

You decide who you see in the mirror, and you only.

## ADJUSTING THE LEVELS

There's a science to getting the perfect shade when coloring hair. You must choose the right developer volume when mixing bleach to get the proper lift. Then you have to choose the right toner to neutralize the unwanted undertones. It's all about adjusting the levels to achieve the desired color.

You instinctively adjust your levels every day. You salt your food. You change out of the shirt with that one loose seam that feels weird. You avoid what annoys you and move toward what you enjoy.

Why is it so hard to adjust the noise levels inside your head?

The world is loud. The noise of social media, your environment, and the voices around you is inescapable. The noise messes with your ability to see yourself accurately.

You're constantly bombarded with images of impossible beauty, success, curated perfection, and triumphant announcements. The world now emphasizes external appearances and accomplishments over all else. Internalizing unrealistic expectations is as common and instinctive as breathing.

You carry these unrealistic expectations based on arbitrary comparisons, and then wonder why you feel like shit.

It's your responsibility to adjust your levels and protect yourself from negativity and self-criticism. When you catch your reflection—whether in a bathroom mirror, a store window, or the front-facing camera on your phone—focus on one positive thing. Don't pick apart the things you don't like or need to improve. Find one positive—just one. Then compliment yourself.

I do this all the time, and it silences my Personal Hater and quiets that gnawing insecurity in my stomach. For example: this morning, to fend off my insecurities about the scar above my lip (which is often the first thing I see in the mirror), and feeling out of sorts because I haven't been to the gym because I've been traveling with a client, I complimented myself on:

- This shade of blue that I'm wearing makes my eyes pop.
- I have a warm smile.
- My hair is falling just right today.
- These jeans fit well and make my legs look athletic.
- My skin looks hydrated.

I used to be so programmed to find every flaw and imperfection. Now instead, I look for the good parts and say, I FUCKING SEE YOU.

If you don't rewrite the code for your brain and cancel your inner critic, it will keep running the same bad program corrupted by the same toxic virus. If you're looking for proof that you are unworthy, unattractive, or undeserving, you'll always find it.

You're the one writing the code. You're the one adjusting the levels to look first, and foremost, for proof of your worth, beauty, and greatness. Let that become the loudest voice in your head, the strongest tone in your color.

# 3.

# You Are the Message and the Messenger in the Marketing of You

*What You're Saying Without Opening Your Mouth*

From a young age, I was captivated by style—not just fashion but the way people presented themselves to the world. It was more than just clothing; it was an unspoken language and visual storytelling. I could see how someone's style or image influenced how others perceived and responded to them.

I remember riding the bus once and watching people come and go on the street, each one making an impression before they even spoke. There was one woman who stood out in particular. She was the epitome of elegance—her raven-brown hair was immaculately groomed, her short red nails were polished to perfection. She wore a bold red coat with a matching hat, her lips were painted in the same striking shade, a bright flash of color against her fair skin. She looked like she had stepped straight out of a Tom Ford campaign. The way she moved, the way she sat down and adjusted her purse exuded confidence and sophistication. I was mesmerized.

That moment stuck with me because it was the first time I truly recognized the power of visual communicating. She wasn't just wearing clothes; she was creating a character, an identity, a presence.

Growing up, we didn't have much money. Luxury brands and designer clothes weren't within reach, but that didn't stop me from experimenting with my own sense of style. I understood early on that presentation mattered—not just for vanity, but for the way it made you feel and the way it shaped the way others treated you.

Every bit of money I earned from working in the salon as a teenager, sweeping up hair and doing small tasks, I saved. Instead of spending it on games or movies, I went to the secondhand shops, carefully selecting pieces that I felt spoke to the person I wanted to become.

Presentation was everything to me. I remember piecing together outfits with the same level of thought and attention as a stylist working on a fashion editorial. I loved wearing waistcoats because they made me feel professional, like I was already in the world I aspired to be part of. A silk shirt, pleated trousers—I dressed with intention, always wanting to present myself as someone who meant business. Looking back, I probably dressed more professionally as a teenager than I do now. But at the time, it wasn't just about looking good; it was about feeling ready, feeling like I belonged in the world of style and fashion.

I was fascinated by how a simple change in clothing could shift perception. A haircut, a tailored suit, the right accessories—these weren't just superficial details; they were tools of transformation.

I realized that how you present yourself can open doors, change conversations, and even alter how you feel about yourself.

That understanding became the foundation of everything I would go on to do. Whether styling a client, creating a look for a red-carpet moment, or crafting my own image, it all came back to the same principle:

*Presentation is power.*

It's the first thing people see before they know anything about you. It's the silent introduction you give to the world. And from the very beginning, I knew I wanted to master that art.

Unless you are a technophobe who doesn't own a computer or a smartphone, every device you use tracks and markets you every moment of every day. Every habit and interest is collected as data from the websites you visit, the social media accounts you engage with, and what you buy as a consumer—even what you hover over and *think* about buying.

Anything that piques your interest is noted as data, then all the marketing and advertising algorithms do their thing. Your feeds, explore pages, and suggestions are altered to influence your engagement and spending. Companies know that our brains can process visual information in as little as thirteen milliseconds. You can assess and make a decision to swipe left, right, up, or down in the blink of an eye—because that's how fast impressions are made.

*Am I interested?* It forces you to ask yourself. *Do I want to see more?*

You make the same snap assessments with every person you encounter in the physical world as you do in the digital world.

*Am I interested? Do I want to know more?*

The same is being done about you.

Society has a funny relationship with the idea of our "looks." The dialogue usually feels negative. Maybe you're the kind of person for whom your outward appearance feels like an afterthought—a burden you don't want to bother with or "that extra thing" you need to tend to. Or maybe it's more of a guilty pleasure: a nice suit jacket for your occasional splurge, or that extra hour you allow yourself to spend getting ready for your annual holiday party.

Maybe it even feels wrong. Shouldn't it be *what's inside* that matters, you ask?

Of course, but that's not how life works. People first notice and are attracted to you based on their first impression of how you present yourself, your energy, vibe, confidence, and appearance—before they get to the deeper, more personal you that's behind all those things.

And why think in such binaries anyway? Is the gorgeous interior of your home a reason for you to neglect the front porch where people enter? Maybe it's time for you to declutter, wash a window, get rid of some of those empty Amazon boxes piling up. Or treat yourself to a new welcome mat.

Think about this: Have you ever been out for coffee and played that game from the rom-coms where you make up backstories for people? You spot someone and instantly start crafting a story—based on their body language, style, and engagement with the world. *She's an insurance adjuster who hates her job but loves making pottery stamped with profane words.* You get the idea.

Now flip it—what story would someone tell you about *you*? If a stranger saw you sitting at a café, what vibe would they pick up? Would they see someone interesting, self-assured, and magnetic? Would they see leading-character energy?

Or would their eyes skim right past you?

Like it or not, first impressions can tell a big story, and it happens fast. Science backs this up—within seconds of meeting someone, our brains start forming opinions based purely on what we *see*. And those first impressions don't just stay surface level. They ripple into everything else.

This is called the *halo effect*—when someone gives off a strong, put-together, confident presence, people tend to assume the best about them in *every* area. Smart. Capable. Trustworthy. Meanwhile, the opposite happens too—the *horns effect* (yes, named after devil horns, and no, I'm not making this up). If someone gives off a disorganized, sloppy, or disengaged vibe, people unconsciously attach that impression to their entire personality.

Whether you like it or not, the billboard of who you are—the walking, talking advertisement for the consumer product of You—shapes how people see you professionally, socially, romantically, and even in ways that might feel unfair.

And here's the thing: In life, we control almost nothing. The one thing we *do* have control over? Ourselves. The way we show up. The way we carry our personalities. The way we present ourselves.

So many of my clients and friends shrug this off. With the wave of a hand, they dismiss any significance we attach to our first impressions, our energies, or appearances as simply shallow or toxic, or something they shouldn't "have" to worry about.

But think about it this way: when you give up and stop caring, you're handing over one of the only things you can actually control.

You are a living marketing campaign for *yourself*. What are you saying without words?

Are you the type of person people can't help but be drawn to?

Do you give off confidence, intrigue, and "I have my life together" energy?

Or are you accidentally sending the message that you'd rather disappear into the background or not be noticed at all?

## PEOPLE CAN'T SEE YOUR INSIDES (SO LET'S TALK ABOUT YOUR OUTSIDES)

Who's your favorite artist? What's your mom like? How many classic novels do you own? How often have you burned the roof of your mouth on pizza because it's your favorite comfort food and patience isn't your thing?

Hate to break it to you, but no one can see any of that.

All the fascinating, weird, fabulous pieces that make up *you*— your sharp wit, impeccable taste in music, and thoughts that keep you up at night—are utterly invisible to most of the world. Only a select few will get the whole experience of who you are. And while *"looks shouldn't matter"* is a sweet idea, let's be honest: they do.

But this reality doesn't always have to be a bad thing. Just because looks matter doesn't mean they're the *only* thing that matters.

I've spent over two decades immersed in the visual language of personal style. And I can tell you one thing for sure—fighting the fact that people make snap judgments based on appearance is a waste of energy. It's human nature. Instead of resisting it, why not use it to your advantage?

## BRANDING ISN'T FAKE—IT'S YOU WITH A STORY TO TELL

When you think of the words *"Personal Branding,"* it's hard to control the impulse to recoil. It's a term that feels reserved for celebrities and influencers trying to sell you the collagen supplement they can't live without or the hair oil that changed their lives.

It feels forced and sales-y, something for the ultrafamous or professionally attractive. But if you're not in some form of entertainment, you probably don't think of personal branding as something for you or that you would ever need.

You're wrong. It's already happening, whether you like it or not.

Much of our interaction is becoming digital thanks to remote work, Zoom meetings, dating apps, and social media. Your presence online and offline matters more than ever. A well-curated appearance can help build a strong personal brand, making you memorable and influential. What does your Zoom background convey? Is it a peek into a cluttered, unkempt home or office or is it a portal into a curated space that shows your style? Does your LinkedIn page highlight your accomplishments, feature an appropriate and flattering photo, and give a glimpse of your writing style? Is your social media capturing your essence, or is it just a dumping ground of aesthetically pleasing cityscapes and sunsets?

Instead of thinking of branding as something foolish, vain, or beyond your scope and ability, think of it strictly as: a messenger for quality. The quality of you, specifically.

A strong personal brand isn't about keeping up false personas and pretending to be some impossibly perfect version of yourself that you're not. It's the opposite: it's making sure people see you for WHO YOU ARE.

Branding is a way to harness what makes you singular. It's a way to balance authenticity with intentionality.

When someone sits in my chair, I ask them a straightforward question:

*What story do you want to tell?*

Because whether you realize it or not, you're already telling a narrative about who you are, last weekend at your party, this morning at work, even right this very moment. Why not make it a good one? The goal isn't to be invisible, it's to be unforgettable to the right people.

And if you don't tell the story about yourself, others will tell it for you—and they might not get it right.

So, what story is it going to be?

How do you carry yourself, what is your energy or vibe? Are your shoulders back, chin up, exuding confidence? Do you look people in the eye and smile warmly? Or are you deliberately unapproachable because you are discerning and not looking to widen your circle? Are you vibrating with enthusiasm and gusto, or focused and serious in your manner?

Let's go back to the coffee shop game, and say you're playing it on a first date. You see one person clearly having a business meeting: their shoulders are a bit hunched, they're fiddling nervously with their hair, averting their eyes, chewing on their lip. They are broadcasting a lot of information. They're uncomfortable, socially anxious, and either don't want to be there, or feel like they don't belong there.

Believe me, I have been this person. Especially when I first came to America, was trying to make a name for myself, find a community, and make friends. I would go out and be signaling to the room, *I'm nobody. Don't look this way. Not sure why I'm even here.*

You scan the coffee shop and see someone else who, though standing alone, is looking around, taking it all in, bobbing their head to the music, drinking their iced coffee with a soft, approachable smile on their face. This person exudes a sense of openness and being socially comfortable that makes you wonder, *What's their life like?*

Your essence fills the space around you. You decide whether it's an inviting and intriguing energy or a force field.

Let me tell you something that I've noticed about Kim Kardashian in the many years I've worked with her. She says hello and introduces herself to everyone in the room. Whether you're the lighting person, the cousin of the PA who brings the coffee order, or the prime minister, no matter who it is, she takes the time to recognize everyone. She doesn't have to; no one expects that of anyone, much less her. It would be easier not to take the time; she is the single busiest person I have ever met, but she makes the effort, and it goes a long way.

Kim has such a big presence; the whole world is fascinated by her. One of the most powerful things she exudes is her genuine kindness and warmth. Her energy is magnetic.

## YOUR LOOK IS YOUR BRAND: OWN THE TOOLS

Social media has turned beauty into an extreme sport—filters, AI, photo editing—people no longer look like people. On one hand, it's exhausting.

On the other hand, we've never had more access to tools that allow us to present ourselves exactly how we want. The playing field has leveled. What's available to the rich and famous is available to all of us now.

Again, let's think of your appearance as your personal marketing campaign. It's not about vanity—it's about strategy. Your look, style, your habits, and presence are extensions of who you are, tools for self-expression, and, most importantly, a concrete way you can attract the life, opportunities, and people you *want* to be around.

You get one physical body in this lifetime. Why not use everything you have to level up—on your terms—exactly how you personally want to be? When you are aligned with your external presentation, your life flows better.

Please don't misunderstand what I'm saying. This is not about cramming yourself into some typical beauty standard or trying to look like someone else. The goal is to amplify what's *already* there and make it authentic to you. Genuine confidence comes from embracing what makes *you* different, what works for you, and makes you feel strong.

Be *your* version of an undeniable presence.

When you stop treating your appearance like an afterthought or a guilty pleasure and start using it as a tool? That's when everything changes.

*Branding yourself is taking control of how you are presented to the world.*

Look at Karl Lagerfeld, Anna Wintour, Steve Jobs, David Bowie, and Lady Gaga—nothing about their personal brands is accidental. Each one of these people inspires complete confidence in what they're doing. No one questions the choices of Diane Keaton, Beyoncé, Zendaya, Jenna Ortega, Tyler, the Creator, Taylor Swift, J Lo, Rihanna, ASAP Rocky, Ayo Edibiri, Reese Witherspoon, Billie Eilish, Doechii, Emma Stone, Pharrell, or Kim Kardashian.

Whether it's a new album, movie, clothing line, product launch, or sound bite from these people—we already know it will be excellent or iconic. And it's not just because they're famous or beautiful. It's because they put something out into the world.

They have repeatedly shown up in certain ways that are particular to them—they create a signature—and they do that consistently. That consistent, cohesive image, which we understand and associate with them, builds trust. They take big swings and have earned respect.

Their personal brand is a promise, and they deliver every time.

I'm not suggesting that everyone needs to become an icon or trendsetter. However, taking control of your brand means taking control of your messaging to be clear, intentional, and aligned with who you are.

It's how you carry and present yourself, what you stand for, and finding a visual language that best represents you.

## WHAT PERSONALITY IS YOUR BRAND PROJECTING RIGHT NOW?

In your life, you send the first message before you even open your mouth. Before a stranger even speaks at a party, you size them up: their outfit, their facial expression, their posture, their makeup, their style of greeting, their tattoos or jewelry, their arrival time, what they're doing with their hands, who they came with, what mood they're exuding.

That's just how our brains are wired as data collectors. We judge books by their covers. Yes, we shouldn't, but we all do because the cover cues information into our brains. You see a thing and you have a feeling about it.

Your brand and style can create business opportunities, like getting you to the right room with the hiring manager or financial backer for your newest endeavor. It can help you attract better romantic and friendship prospects, communicate your values and ambitions, and help you stand out in competitive environments.

Here are a few examples of what internal traits can be communicated by different styles:

- Tailored & Polished communicates, *"I'm sophisticated, competent, and reliable. I pay attention to detail and plan ahead and take things seriously."*
- Clean & Casual communicates, *"I'm approachable, trustworthy, and easygoing. I can pivot when needed."*
- Bold, Attention Grabbing & Trendy communicates, *"I'm a risk taker, a little edgy, and always up for something new."*
- Understated & Minimal communicates, *"I'm classic, discerning, and not swayed by trends."*

What does your style and energy say about you? Does it match who you are?

## HOW TO DETERMINE AND DEFINE YOUR VISUAL STYLE

If you don't know where to start or you think this is beyond you, it's okay. Don't worry. You're not expected to get a whole new wardrobe or suddenly have the savvy or skills of an off-duty model. Here's what I suggest.

1. **You study.** Put in the time, effort, and research like anything else you aspire to. Whose style do you admire? Who gives you that pang of envy? Who are they? How do they present? What do you respond to?
2. **Build a visual file.** Create a list, make a photo album on your phone, a file on your desktop, fill it with pictures of anything that excites you—attitudes, art, fashion, hair, makeup looks, jobs, moods—basically anything that makes you feel something.
3. **Look for patterns.** (Now we're talking!) What are the recurring themes behind what you're drawn to

repeatedly? These are all indicators of what you want
for yourself.

4. **Try things on.** I mean that both literally and
   figuratively. Style isn't only about what looks good,
   it's about what makes you feel powerful, invincible,
   bursting with uncontainable joy. See what fits you
   physically and emotionally. Try out a new way of
   greeting people. Don't be the one who moves out
   of the way when an oncoming pedestrian is headed
   straight at you. Take the scenic and more interesting
   path, even if it adds five minutes to your commute.

5. **Commit, but also evolve.** What do you want to try
   next? Go with it, and feel free to adapt it later. Your
   personal brand shouldn't be set in stone. It should
   grow with you. Consistency builds recognition, so
   find your lane and mess around with it.

*The only limits are the ones you set.*

We live in a golden age of personal style where trends are being rewritten constantly by people of all shapes and sizes. There
is no mold you are expected to fit into. The only limits you have
are a lack of willingness and imagination. With intention and
execution come great returns.

First impressions matter, obviously, and yes, you only get
one chance to send that first message or make that first impact.
But life gives you second and third chances. How many times
have you said to someone or someone has told you, *"You're not
who I thought you'd be when we first met,"* or *"You're not at all like
I assumed you'd be when I first saw you."*

Impressions change with new information, and life is long enough that fate puts people in your path to give you multiple chances if you don't get it right the first time.

Once social media became a thing, I began using it as an opportunity to show my portfolio. I was, and still am, consistently showing my work and broadcasting the evolution of my abilities and my personal brand. While you might argue that social media shouldn't be a big focus, the truth is that you never know who might be watching you and making their first impressions.

When someone from Jennifer Lopez's team initially emailed me, I thought it was spam. I didn't even respond. Then they reached out again and asked if I was available to do her hair in Las Vegas for her residency. I was still living in Leicester at the time, so I wasn't able to take the job—but the idea that, had I been able to get to Las Vegas quickly, I would have booked a job with Jennifer Lopez created a spark.

I decided I needed to move to America if I wanted to make my career really happen.

A month later, I packed two suitcases and moved to Los Angeles on Christmas Eve. The phone didn't ring for the first few months, and I even found myself starting to run out of money. America was a big place and I felt very small, but I finally booked my first job. A short time after that, J Lo's team reached out again. This time it was to style her new music video. I was ecstatic. A call was scheduled to go over the "creative" with her team, so I knew what looks I needed to prepare for the job.

The day of the call, someone rang me and as soon as I answered, they said they were just going to put me through to Jennifer.

Jennifer? As in Jennifer Lopez? My mind raced. What do I call her? Jennifer? J Lo? Jenny from the Block? And then suddenly Jennifer Lopez was there on the other end of the line.

"Hey, baby," she said. "Here's what we're doing . . ."

I couldn't believe I was on the phone with J Lo.

She was warm, lovely, and clear about what she wanted for the music video concept. When I hung up the phone . . . I couldn't remember most of what she said because I was in such a state of shock.

I left no stone unturned. I needed to have every possible option ready for any look she could want for the "Ain't Your Mama" music video shoot. I still have the picture of all the wigs I prepared for that shoot lined up in my modest studio apartment.

When I finally did meet J Lo, the day of the shoot, one of the first things she said to me was, "I've had my eye on you for a while, and I knew you were the right person for the job."

She meant my social media. My portfolio. She had somehow found me or been exposed to my feed, thought I had talent, liked my work, and reached out me. I missed my first chance to work with J Lo back in Vegas, but because of the first impression I left, I was given a second chance with this job. We have worked together consistently ever since.

This kind of alignment of the stars doesn't always happen. But that doesn't mean you should rush to abandon your brand when the stars don't align or just because you had a shitty first—or third or tenth—impression. Give yourself the grace. There are always opportunities to switch gears, continue to evolve, and tell a new story about yourself, even to your friends or people you've known your whole life.

And there's still a whole world full of people who have yet to get to have a first impression of you.

# 4.

# The Power and Influence of Hair

## *How Your Locks Can Hold the Key to Your Confidence*

I started doing wigs in the salon when I was twenty-one. I hadn't been drawn to wigs before, but a few clients, strong, confident women I knew well, came to the salon with cancer diagnoses. They were like rabbits in the headlights: scared, stunned, frozen. They knew that the cancer treatment would eventually take their hair, if it hadn't already.

It was wild as a young hair stylist to see these very established and empowered women unravel before my eyes and look so lost. In the space of nine months, I remember I had three different clients say to me that they'd rather lose their breasts than their hair. Their chests they could conceal from the world in boxy jackets or oversized sweaters, but their hair? That they couldn't hide.

I realized that it was not just being sick or going through something internal that was upsetting to my clients—it was that everyone could *see* that they were sick. Losing their hair was losing their privacy over what they were going through. It was the constant reminder of being sick because of the way people treated them. That was one of the biggest things they struggled with.

Wigs supplied to cancer patients through the National Health Service came from medical suppliers, not beauty suppliers. They were thick, unnatural, mostly acrylic or acrylic blends, so they looked almost costumey, and were very obviously wigs—nothing like the seamless ones we have now that have more human hair content or better synthetics and look so realistic that no one can tell. The technology has advanced and the evolutions of wigs is significant from those first wigs I worked with.

I made it my mission to style the wigs to make them look more natural. I plucked the hairline with tweezers one hair at a time and colored the wig's roots to match the color closer to what my client's hair had been like.

Watching these women walk out of the salon feeling confident that they could own and control this particular part of their cancer—that it was theirs to share if and when they wanted to, and not something automatically known to a stranger on the street—this confirmed that what I was doing was important. The time I invested working on those wigs was more meaningful than I had realized. The women's gratitude for giving them back their sense of self and privacy, by making their illness more invisible when they wanted it to be, will stay with me forever.

That experience fueled my ambition to master the art of wigs, which require their own education. I went to London and New York and took classes, working in the theater and film hair departments to learn the intricacies of wigs and what works and translates for stage and screen.

Laying a wig to look undetectable is quite a process. Most wigs and extensions don't come in the precise shade you want, so I learned to color them. A wig became a blank canvas that I could transform into something unique. I became obsessed, and they unlocked a whole level of what I could do as a stylist.

At the time, I hadn't understood how many people wear wigs every day, or that there was any kind of stigma to wearing wigs. I didn't know that wearing a wig was something that a lot of people tried to keep hidden. I love that so many beautiful women and celebrities wear them with unabashed pride.

They're an essential and vibrant element of hair culture, pop culture, fashion, and art.

Wigs and extensions are now a massive part of my styling practice. I have an entire area of my hair studio dedicated to them. The quality, realism, and comfort of them are incredible. They're virtually undetectable.

I've found so much joy in crafting glamorous, edgy, and iconic looks with wigs and extensions for some of my most prominent clients: Kim Kardashian's neon green wig to match her Lamborghini in Miami, Jennifer Lopez's pastel mermaid and blonde blunt bob with floral stencil for her "In The Morning" music video, Dua Lipa's Barbiecore Pink locks to match her Puma collection campaign, and Katy Perry's beachy blonde wave wig that broke the internet after a long stint with a platinum pixie cut. Preparing wigs in advance for a shoot or an event and having multiple hair looks ready in minutes is a game-changer.

The great thing about wigs, extensions, and pieces is that you can try things out before you make significant changes to your hair. You can buy clip-on bangs and ponytails online and have them delivered in a few days. You can order multiple wigs before changing your look completely, if only just to scratch the itch or boost the ego with no downside. It's that easy.

The best part of working with wigs for me still is the moment when someone going through hair loss or alopecia gets to see themselves with beautiful, realistic hair. There's nothing like it. It takes me back to being twenty-one, utterly unaware that much of my own growth would come from working with hair that doesn't grow.

It was when I started working on wigs for these clients that my eyes were opened to how significant our hair can be. It's so much more than the strands of keratin on your head. Hair has immense cultural and personal significance. It's a statement expressing your identity, a message you send the world before you open your mouth. It speaks of where you come from, who you are, or want to be.

Hair is one of the great identifiers we carry through life:

*"Do you know Sasha?"*

*"Is she the blonde woman? Wavy hair to her shoulders?"*

*"No, she's the one with a long straight hair, more chocolate brown."*

Hair is the first defining detail used when describing a person (usually followed by height, but my services sadly don't include changes in that arena). The memorability of your hair constantly qualifies you to other people, whether you realize it or not.

It can frame you, reveal you, or shield you, make you feel seen or help you disappear. It's a source of pride and self-consciousness. It's a medium for reinvention and aspiration. Hair can feed into your idea of your beauty or status. It's one of the ways we remember our life; a heritage trait we pass down and receive from our family.

Hair also marks time and holds memory. Ask anyone who's ever grown out a lousy chapter of their life. A man who shaves his head after years of fighting his thinning hair or receding hairline, after years of pretending to be someone he's not. A person cutting their hair to reflect their true gender. Someone finally able to grow hair after cancer treatment. The weight they feel lifted isn't just physical—it's capital *E, Emotional*. It's a seismic event.

Everyone is obsessed with their hair (or lack thereof). The time you spend thinking about your hair, when added up, would probably shock you if calculated. When you think of influential, successful, magnetic people, their hair is as recognizable as their faces. Look at Anna Wintour. Her iconic bob is as sharp as her editorial genius.

So what's my point in saying all of this?

Let's think of your hair as both a starting point for the kind of transformation you want to introduce into your life. What's your attitude toward your own hair? Mostly negative or positive, and why? What are your habits around it? What's the message about you that it's sending?

If hair holds this much significance over this many areas of our lives, think of all that could be possible when you change just one thing about it. What could it unleash?

When I was nine, I did my mum's hair for the first time. We didn't have much growing up (more on that later), but my mum grew up even poorer than we did, and her opportunity for a normal childhood was cut short. I had this desire to make her look and feel something she'd never been given the chance to feel—glamorous.

I'll never forget the moment she stood up and looked in the mirror. Her entire energy shifted. For a split second, she forgot she was a mother of five trying to make ends meet and run a household in dreary Leicester. She saw someone different—someone she had always been, but was never allowed to become. The person she never had the opportunity to discover because of her circumstances. She saw herself as Jane. Not as a wife, mother, or orphan, but as the person she hadn't carved out any room for.

It's funny looking back at old photos of all the things I used to do to her hair—Egyptian-inspired Cleopatra bangs to big, editorial curls—because I now realize how much those moments shaped me. My mum was always in the chair, my model, letting me experiment, practice, and become who I was meant to be despite what my circumstances dictated.

I distinctly remember watching her transform and thinking, *This is my superpower.*

With my mum as my muse, I proved to myself what I'd always instinctively felt: hair is an art form. Changing it should be as natural as changing your clothes—another extension of self-expression. It shouldn't be shocking if someone goes from long to short or brunette to pink.

At nine years old, I doubt this was something I could articulate, but it felt like a natural understanding back then. It was never about, *let's just cut my mum's hair off and be crazy*. It was about making my "mum" even more "herself" to me—who she was, who she wanted to be, who she *could* be.

When I gave her an updo to make her look like a glamorous star, it was like I had bewitched her with a joie de vivre. She felt cool and pretty, not tied so tightly to the domestic identity of her life. She wore her favorite blouse that she usually saved for special occasions, and I would catch her looking at herself in mirrors, posing for herself. It was a carefree, flirty confidence I hadn't seen on Mum before.

From then on, hair became my medium for uncovering hidden identities and making them shine. From when my mum was my only client to my first salon job when I was thirteen to my last *Vogue* cover, I have witnessed firsthand how hair can reinvigorate the human spirit.

## SEE THE OPPORTUNITY, NOT THE INSECURITY

When someone sits in my chair, they relinquish control and place their faith in my hands. What we do together in this intimate setting and that moment is never *just* about the hair—it's about transformation.

I don't mean that in a pompous or glib way; I mean it literally. Hair can truly be the difference between a good day and a bad one, walking into a room feeling refreshed with potential or held back by old habits. Between possibilities and insecurities.

Aside from special events, people book hair appointments when they need a shield, a repair, or a rebirth. When someone tells me, "I could never pull that off," my first question is, "Who told you that?"

Nine out of ten times, it's no one—just a belief they've carried for years, something they've accepted without question, even though it probably has no basis in fact.

I have a client who has a beautiful, thick head of naturally curly hair. She always refers to it as "unruly." She can never get it to cooperate; it takes half a bottle of leave-in conditioner to get a comb through it; she can't go anywhere humid or it's unmanageable.

Because of this, the amount of hostility she has for her hair or how limited she feels because of it is abnormally amplified in my opinion. She always wants me to blow her hair straight or bring down the volume. I remember doing her hair for a daytime For Your Consideration awards event. Her look was a structured suit with cigarette pants, classic Louboutin stiletto pumps, and delicate diamond and gold jewelry. She wanted me to tame her unruliness into a slicked-back low bun.

"Do you know how many people I have to put a head full of extensions on to get your volume?" I told her. "I find your hair to be really exciting and not at all unruly."

"Well, you didn't grow up in my house where my mom complained every day about having to brush the knots out."

Of course, she hated her hair: she was given the message daily that it was bad, a problem, or something shameful. She adopted that point of view because it was drilled into her.

"This is my area. I know hair, and yours is not unruly, it's just opinionated. And your mother wasn't using the right products or approach to work with your texture and thickness."

Because her public look was so polished, I convinced her to let me make her hair the focus instead of hiding it away. I assured her that what she had on her head was actually a gold mine. Something that could be unforgettable and impactful. Instead of a ladylike ballerina bun, I diffused her hair to enhance the curls and volume until she had a gorgeous mane.

When she assessed herself in the mirror with her hair, makeup, and wardrobe all done, she literally giggled, "This is a MOMENT."

It was a fashion moment for sure. But it was also a moment of her letting go of the bitterness and limitations that her hair had represented.

My job is to help people get to the core of who they are and strip away their limitations. I'm here to show them they *can* let go and redefine themselves, starting with their haircut, but crucially reaching far beyond it.

If someone is uncomfortable with their appearance, it shows. In these moments, whether their best friend or the entire room or the red carpet tells them they look fantastic, it doesn't matter. If the person isn't feeling it, they won't own it. Confidence isn't just in the cut, color, or style; it's in the emotions they carry about themselves.

I always tell my clients: confidence is a muscle that needs to be exercised to grow stronger. They just need to look at themselves and see *opportunities*, not insecurities.

## FROM THE OUTER TO THE INNER

Picture yourself in my chair, looking into the mirror. This moment is powerful. You're not just open to change *but asking for it*. You're looking at yourself honestly, maybe noticing things you've always critiqued in the past, but also knowing *it's about to improve*.

You can feel the optimism lift through your whole body. The anticipation alone raises your energy. Even before a single strand has been touched, there's already a visceral brightening from being able to picture the future improvement.

Now, imagine what can happen after the cut—after you move with actual intention.

When a client goes for a drastic change—bold color, a daring cut—it's rarely about aesthetics and more often a symbolic metamorphosis. They're not just changing their hair; they're stepping out of stagnancy into something new. They're answering the latent call for bravery they might have just shoved down and ignored for too long.

When I spin them in the chair, I watch their confidence rise in real time as they reconnect with a part of themselves they'd forgotten or had simply let atrophy.

I've seen my clients get a sleek bob and look in the mirror, finally able to visualize themselves walking into the boardroom and giving that big client pitch they've been having stress dreams about. I've seen clients get a killer blowout and feel inspired to go flirt with the regular at bar trivia night they've been too shy to talk to.

I know, I know: changing your hair is easy, but changing your life is not. But still, there's something potent in this feeling of anticipation that I want us to hold on to. When you undergo an outward change, you have an internal response: you look and feel different.

That feeling can carry you much farther than you realize.

**5.**

# The Other Four-Letter F-Word That's Holding You Back

*You Deserve Much Better
than Settling for "Fine"*

"It's fine" is possibly the single most overused sentence in the English language. At best, it's a neutral placeholder that virtually means nothing—and at worse, it's something we say even when we don't mean it, when it absolutely isn't fine. While I'm sure we could spend several pages on the implications of this for our modern society, I want to ask a more pressing question: When did we decide we're all so okay with things being fine?

*"How's your cold chicken piccata tonight?"*

*"It's fine."*

*"How are your lopsided bangs that are two inches shorter than you wanted?"*

*"It's fine."*

*"Sorry, I'm forty minutes late."*

*"It's fine."*

"It's fine" is what you say when you lack the courage to ask for what you want. "It's fine" teaches those around you that you don't need their best and will settle for whatever you get instead.

*Fine* is a purgatory of your own choosing. It's the mindset that keeps you chugging along on cruise control, never actually advocating for yourself. It's code for: "it's not worth it," "I don't have the energy to get into why it's NOT fine," "I'll deal with whatever this is since I can't get what I actually want," "Everyone else is fine with it and I don't want to be the asshole," and a million more variations of you not getting the level, quality, respect, and action you deserve.

But why do you feel powerless to question what happened when something goes wrong?

Because it's easier? Because conflict is terrifying?

It's absolutely not fine, so stop saying it is. Do you know how many people have come to me with a terrible haircut, asking me to fix what someone else has done to them? Hundreds. I always ask them, "Why didn't you speak up and stop it while it was happening? Or ask the hairdresser to fix it?" They shrug sheepishly. "It's fine. It'll grow out." Even worse, I had a client tell me they didn't stop the hairdresser from cutting her hair too short because she *"DIDN'T WANT TO HURT HER HAIR-DRESSER'S FEELINGS!"* That is complete madness.

Do you know what that tells me? That they've been settling for "fine" in every other area of their lives, too. They're not just letting themselves get a bad haircut. *They're letting their whole life happen to them* and just . . . going along with it. The marketing job they hate, the on-again-off-again best friend that's hurting them, that goal to open a little antique shop that they never achieve—those things are all "fine."

But they're not.


By the most true and literal definition, "fine" is supposed to mean quality and excellence—fine arts, fine wine, fine dining.

~~~~~~~~~~~~~~~~

*Instead, we use "fine" as permission*
*for mediocrity—or worse.*

~~~~~~~~~~~~~~~~

Don't you want excellent, or at minimum, better? I do and I think you should, too.

The great malaise of our time is that we accept less than we want or deserve from everyone, including ourselves, often because it's the path of least resistance. It's an epidemic of settling. You sidestep opportunities, afraid of conflict or rejection if you speak up. You stay silent when people ask so that you won't be seen as problematic or annoying. You don't want to rock the boat for fear you won't be invited to sail again. But maybe "not sailing again" isn't even as scary as you think.

What is the worst that can happen if you speak up and call it what it is? What will it take to admit that something is disappointing, inconsiderate, or not what you wanted? How affected do you need to be before you tell the truth?

In a life that's built on "fine," you settle safely into your comfort zone, where nothing changes and everything stays the same. Is the comfort zone cozy? A hundred percent, yes. Is it fulfilling? Not really.

Comfort doesn't lead to growth. It's a nice place to catch your breath and watch a movie every now and then, but in the long run, it keeps you stagnant, stuck, and bored if not dull.

Is that what you want written in your obituary when your time's up?

*"She always said it was fine even when it wasn't, and she never got the life she wanted. After the service, a reception will be held with*

*bland, cold, and tasteless appetizers. By her own account, they will be fine."*

Fine is a safe word, and that's precisely the problem. If you keep living for the "fine" moments, you'll never get the WOW ones.

When you open up room in your life for the tensions that could arise from pushing back your best, that's when everything starts to shift for you. Your mindset, boundaries, and expectations. You will attract people, situations, and opportunities that reflect your true worth. You will *level up*.

You won't be afraid to voice your needs because you know that you are the one who loses when you feign satisfaction.

If all you aspire to is for your life to be passable, you're holding the wrong book. Fine is the easy way out—and that roadmap isn't one you'll find here.

## CHALLENGE OF THE DAY

I want you to put a hair tie or elastic on your wrist and snap it every time you say the word "fine" today.

In fact, what I really want is for you to stop saying, "it's fine" as a reflexive habit even when it isn't. But since habits take time to break, try snapping your hair tie each time you do it. The snap will make you more aware of the individual decisions—big and small—that you make daily, without even registering it, where you're sacrificing the excellence you deserve.

The next time someone asks how something is that IS NOT FINE, find a comfortable way to tell them. Here are a few for you to try on for size.

"It falls a little short for me."

"Not going to lie, I'm finding this a challenge."

"There's room for improvement."

"It's not what I expected, but I'll try to make it work."

"This needs some fine-tuning."

"I appreciate the effort, but it doesn't work for me."

"There might be a better option, let's try to figure one out together."

"I have some concerns."

"I'm not really vibing with this."

"I wish I could say this is fine, but I'm not entirely comfortable with this."

"It's not really up to par. Let's have another go at it."

"Does it look fine to you?"

Life is too short for it to only be serving you "fine." I think you can demand more.

## FINE OR GOOD ENOUGH?

I also believe there's a distinct difference between when something is "fine" and "good enough." Fine accepts without question, where good enough measures and decides. Good enough still might not be exactly what you wanted or how you wanted, but it looks at what you are getting, the circumstances, effort, and then taps into your internal feelings to consider it holistically. Good enough means you can find contentment and satisfaction; fine means you've let go of that expectation.

Next time you're in a situation where you're tolerating something just because it's easier, more comfortable, or because you're avoiding confrontation, ask yourself is it "fine" or "good enough"? If it's the former, stop and speak up. You're not destined just to be fine. You're reaching for greatness.

Settling for less isn't always the problem. For some of us, we're not saying "it's fine" to other people—we're saying it to ourselves.

I have to admit, I lean on this word all the time. If "I'm fine" is always in my back pocket, I don't need to engage with every single person asking me how I'm doing more deeply than a surface level answer. "I'm fine" keeps things simple and lets me go about my day—no awkward oversharing or uncomfortable conversations.

When you slip or fall in public, you jump up and declare to everyone, "I'm fine." Nothing to see here. Everyone move along.

I'm fine. All the time. Thanks for asking.

One day, I was picking up coffee and ran into an old friend I hadn't seen since a celebrity tequila launch. I was in the thick of a challenging split from a partner. I was in a state—numb but also raw, struggling to focus on work, constantly replaying the weeks and conversations leading up to the breakup. I was feeling a lot of things, but fine was not one of them.

Naturally, we exchanged hugs and complimented each other for looking good because it is Los Angeles, and that's part of the social ritual. She asked me how I was, with a concerned furrow of her brows that told me she had heard about my breakup. (You can always tell when someone knows more than they should by the brow—unless they've had too much Botox.)

"I'm fine. So fine. Really. I am completely fine." My words came out cheery and false while my face struggled to maintain the ridiculous smile I was forcing.

"Fuck, I wouldn't be. It sounds awful and I'm so sorry, and I hope you know that you don't have to be okay. No one expects you to be. You can just be fucked-up and going through it and that's okay."

Her concern was so genuine, that my pretense fell. "I'm fine" was what I said to my reflection in the mirror that morning when I was having an anxiety attack. But it was under no circumstances true.

I admitted to my friend that I was "fine" in a *fake it until you make it* way more than a literal one. I knew I would one day be fine, and was leaning into that, trying to speed up getting to actual fine-ness. It felt good to admit the truth.

On my drive home, I couldn't stop thinking about why I was so quick to close a conversation rather than open one. Why did I want to disengage rather than engage with her but more importantly, with myself?

Did I decide to do this at some point in my life, or was this something I was programmed with when I was young? When you're little and you get hurt, sometimes the first thing our mom or dad says to us is, "You're fine." Doesn't matter if you're bleeding or bruised. You're told whatever happened to you, you'll be okay. I'm a father, after all, so I understand the instinct to absolve your child of pain and reinforce their resilience every time they get knocked down.

But what if this phrase also creates a default state of presuming to be fine, unconsciously and without examination, until we're on our knees and can't avoid the pain any longer?

Most people are not fine all the time. Why can't I permit myself to be one of them? What is really behind the deflection of "I'm fine"? Why was I constantly pretending rather than investigating?

Saying, "I'm fine," whether it was me psyching myself up in the mirror or lying to my friend at the coffee shop, was really just me being in complete denial. I wasn't fine, and I shouldn't have been. I had just gone through a traumatic situation. Fine can't be expected. And healing can't happen when you're disconnecting from your feelings, so I dug in.

*How was I, really? Well* . . . I was managing but not much else. I wasn't sleeping, but I wanted to sleep all the time. I couldn't focus on my job but needed to stay busy, yet I was utterly un-motivated. I felt sad, depressed, and nauseated; I was consumed with dread, and felt misunderstood and confused. And I was hiding my pain from my friends and family because none of them really understood why I stayed in the relationship or supported it when the red flags were evident from the start.

*I was not fine but at the same time, I knew I would be . . . with time.*

## ADJUSTING THE LEVELS

You guessed correctly, I'm running it back. Here's another opportunity to adjust the levels and stop saying, "I'm fine." I understand the concern of oversharing and making people un-comfortable or burdened with more than they expected to hear. But they wouldn't have asked if they didn't want to know.

And if a person *is* only asking out of social courtesy, well, their artificiality doesn't mean *we* have to be artificial in our answer.

The next time someone asks how you are, tell them something closer to the truth. Here are a few to get you started but find your version that makes you comfortable and fits your personality.

"I've been better, though right now, it's hard to remember when."

"Only silver lining is this day will be over soon."

"On a scale of one to ten, I'm at a six but only because I'm having a good hair day."

"Hanging in there and clawing my way back."

"Just prepping for my comeback."

"Better than some, not better than others."

"In a bit of a transition phase. I'll keep you posted."

"Holding it together by the power of coffee."

"I'm falling apart in ways I didn't know were possible."

All of these at least have a hint of truth, relieve the burden of lying, and open up to the possibility of a conversation.

## RECLAIMING FINE

Remember how I said that change comes in the small moments where you make a shift that has bigger repercussions? This is one of those things. You can reclaim "fine" to mean what it should. Instead of taking the mediocre as it is, ask yourself, "How can I make this *actually* fine? What can I do to level up this experience so that I feel good about it?" Imagine the massive change to your everyday life if you filled it with things, experiences, and people who are excellent instead of just passable.

Think of a concrete example of the last time you said "I'm fine" or "It's fine" and didn't mean it. What was the real feeling behind your "fine"s? Call it what it is. Be specific.

Understanding why you settle for fine is the key to changing that behavior. If you were sitting in my chair in the studio and we were having an honest conversation, these are the questions I would ask you:

Are you tolerating situations, people, or jobs that make you feel "fine" but not fulfilled or satisfied? If so, why?

What is the one thing in your life that's currently "fine" but could be so much more? It could be your relationship, job, self-care routine, home/living situation, anything.

Can you change your default settings to check in with yourself and ask, "Am I really okay with this?" before saying "I'm fine" or "it's fine"?

What would it look like if it was great?

How would you transform this area of your life if you knew you couldn't fail?

# 6.

# Your Envy Is Not a Monster

*It's Trying to Tell You What You Really Want*

Envy can be agonizing. It crawls under your skin, infects your mind and body, and makes you feel horrible for wanting what someone else has. Getting that gut punch whenever someone else has glossier hair, perfect skin, a better wardrobe, a hotter boyfriend, a cooler job, and VIP wristbands to a life you wish was yours. It's not a subtle feeling. It burns.

Envy whispers, *"How come they get to have it, and I don't?"*

*"I guess you're not as hot as you thought you were."*

*"Look at what they have. Look where they're going. Look who loves them."*

*"You're just not the type of person who gets to have that."*

We're taught that envy is ugly, shameful, something to suppress at all costs. It's the green-eyed monster, one of the seven deadly sins, the sickness of the soul. So of course, it makes sense why would we think envy could have nothing good to offer us.

But what if we're looking at this complex emotion all wrong?

I want to propose that maybe envy isn't there to make you miserable. Maybe it's simply your internal navigation device trying to guide you forward.

Instead of shoving envy down, being ashamed, or pretending you don't feel it, what if you tried listening to it?

*Maybe envy is a flashing arrow pointing
to what could be yours, but you haven't
admitted to yourself that you want it.*

Envy is actually a powerful force for motivation and growth, urging you to close the gap between longing and having. Instead of letting it sit and fester inside us, we should actually listen to that voice saying, *"Psst! Hey! Check this thing out. This might be something you want."*

Start using your envy as a motivator instead of just letting it sabotage you. Are you feeling jealous of someone's career, real estate portfolio, ability to make a plain white T-shirt look like a strong fashion choice? Good. Use it. Once I learned how to listen to my envy and then channel it, I didn't feel powerless. I felt driven.

## HOW TO USE YOUR ENVY
### Step One: Own and Identify Your Envy

Stop pretending you're above it. Everyone feels envy, it's universal. It doesn't make you bad; it makes you human. Be inquisitive. What is the exact thing you're jealous of? Not the surface stuff, the real stuff.

Is it that person on Instagram whose career seems to be enjoying a perpetual five-star holiday? Is it someone you know personally who is thriving in ways you most certainly are not—getting promotions, receiving accolades, having all the luck?

What do you envy? The success? The confidence? The lifestyle? The relationships? And why do you envy these things? Why do you want it?

When I was a few years into my styling career in the salon in England, I got hung up feeling envious about my coworker's higher rates. She charged £20 more than I did and I asked myself, "Why is this bothering me? Why do I want this? Why am I stressing about this?"

I thought about the money. Sure, it was a sizeable difference once I added up how many clients I saw in a week, but it wasn't life-changing money. I realized it was really about the *regard* that she got because of her higher rate. I felt confident that I was at least as good if not a better stylist than her, but she had come from another salon where her rate was established.

I started to feel really resentful at work. It was like I was having a one-sided silent fight with the salon, but the salon didn't know it. One morning I woke up and couldn't take it anymore. I really felt like I would burst if I didn't say anything about it. That day at work, I told the salon managers that I was raising my rate by £20.

You know what happened? They told me to inform reception and my clients of my new rate and didn't bat a lash. My envy had unnecessarily become this big negative storm over me because I had framed it as a negative instead of a motivator.

Once you name it, you take away the negative energy and the power to make you feel small. And sometimes, that requires you reflecting on what it is you really want that's sparking the envy. Because ultimately, even if my salon hadn't let me raise my rate, I could've looked for other ways to achieve the regard I wanted and envied—since that's the thing it was really about.

Instead of simmering with hot envy, reframe that simmer as a focused desire. Ask yourself: What is stopping you from going for it? Is it fear? Doubt? Money? Circumstances? A story you're telling yourself that you're not good enough to get it or have it?

**Step Two: Break It Down and Turn It into a Goal**

The underbelly of envy is an unmet desire tied up in insecurity.

Envy isn't about them. It's about you. The person who has it all holds the mirror, reflecting what you want. Now that you know what you're jealous of, dissect it. Use your envy as a blueprint.

What steps did they take to get there? What skills do they have that you don't? What moves did they make that you haven't? What sacrifices did they make that you're avoiding? How did they build whatever it is that they have?

> *Whenever you feel envious, stop thinking, "Why them?" and start thinking, "Why not me?"*

Maybe the people who have what you want did the work, took the risks, and bet on themselves when no one else did. You can do the same. But, maybe, they got it by sheer randomness, nepotism, chance, or didn't deserve it at all. Life isn't always fair and the playing field isn't always level. Sadly, that is something that you have to suck up and accept. It doesn't mean you stop trying.

**Step Three: Make a Plan, Take a Step**

Sitting in your envy or trying to ignore it isn't productive. The space between wanting and having is filled by action.

Instead of watching what you want from a distance, getting competitive and stewing—get a front row seat. Get close to the people you envy; try getting a lunch with them. Get strategic. Be a goal digger. Surround yourself with betterness. Make strong ties, build them up, and they'll pull you alongside them as they rise.

If you envy someone's promotion or position, investigate what triggered it. Was it a metric or particular performance? Was it negotiated with their boss? What conversations were had behind the scenes to secure it?

If you envy a relationship, turn the lens around and focus on yourself. Are you putting yourself out there? Are you actively being the best version of yourself someone else would want to be with? Are you brave enough to make the changes that attract the kind of partner you want?

Do something that makes you feel closer to getting what you want. Take steps today—small, consistent ones, and then they'll snowball into bigger things as you get more inspired.

The trick is momentum. One small action today leads to another tomorrow. Soon, you will find yourself living instead of envying.

## Step Four: Make It Uniquely Yours

Envy isn't about copying someone else's life. You don't want their exact life. You want the feeling their life gives you. Your envy points toward a version of your dream, not someone else's. It's an inspiration. You want to carve your path, find what lights you up and gives you that feeling, and make it your own.

Your dream won't, and shouldn't, look exactly like anyone else's. Your goal isn't to be them. It's to be the best version of you. This is about taking envy, distilling inspiration and motivation from it, and transforming that into something that can take you somewhere.

I remember a client who came in with a picture of a celebrity with a gorgeous, edgy, long bob. She said, *"I want this. Exactly."*

This client was ten years older than the celebrity in the photo, with entirely different coloring and face shape. The celebrity had olive skin, brown eyes, caramel hair, and a heart-shaped face, and my client had long ash blonde hair with an oval-shaped face.

I asked her what about the hairstyle she was drawn to, and she replied, "You can tell she feels untouchable."

"So it's her confidence that you're vibing with."

"Exactly," she laughed. "I'll have what she's having."

My client knew she wouldn't magically look exactly like this celebrity if she copied her hairstyle, but that's not what she was looking for. It was the confidence and agency this celebrity has. It was the ability to grab onto joy that she was missing or had lost.

I gave her a similar treatment, but tweaked it to better suit her coloring and oval-shaped face. Her hair came out perfect, but it wasn't the exact thing she asked for, because it was her own version of it and not that celebrity's. It was about finding the ingredient that could unlock a part of her that she desperately needed and now saw again in the mirror—she'd made it her own.

### Step Five: Have Gratitude to Balance Your Envy

Gratitude feels like the last thing you can access when envy is clawing away at you, but it keeps you grounded, and a little goes a long way. Think of it like a deep-conditioning treatment for your soul and mindset. It's the difference between feeling inspired and being trapped in victimhood, feeling like life is unfair.

Think of a specific area of your life where you've been feeling envy lately. Maybe it's your job. I want you to make a list of your general "needs" versus "wants" when it comes to that area. Maybe "wants" include: a close commute, friendly coworkers, a salary that allows for an upgrade to your apartment. By contrast, maybe your needs include: covering your baseline bills, or the chance to enjoy weekends without working overtime.

| Needs | Wants |
|-------|-------|
|       |       |
|       |       |
|       |       |

Now, dwell on the "needs" column for a moment. Here, you can see visible proof of what needs are being met instead of obsessing on the "wants" that are not. As long as you are still drawing breath, you have something to be thankful for. Once you start naming one thing you're grateful for, more will appear.

Gratitude doesn't mean you have to pretend you don't want more, but envy without thankfulness will turn to bitterness and resentment without fail. Having or practicing gratitude reminds you that while striving for more, you already have things worth appreciating.

You can be celebrating what you have and still want for more. People who succeed at transforming their envy into reality are the ones who balance their envy with gratitude. Not to mention, they're the ones who channel and radiate positivity and the ones OTHERS end up envying!

The next time you feel that pang of jealousy or thrumming of envy sitting on your chest, turn the feeling into action. Remember, it's just your heart's way of nudging you, daring you to get to work and go for the things you truly want.

### ENVY ANALYSIS

Grab a journal, your notes app, or your laptop. We're digging into your envy.

**The List**

Write down five people who make you feel that pang of jealousy. Be brutally honest. This is just for you; no one else will see it, and you can delete or destroy it later. It could be someone you know, a public figure, or even that annoyingly perfect person from your feed.

**The Why**

Next to each name, write precisely *what* you envy about them. Be specific. Is it their career? Their confidence?

Their love life? Their style? The way they seem to turn every eye when they walk into a room? Pinpoint it.

### The Translation

Now, for each thing you envy, flip it around into a personal insight.

If you envy someone's career success, maybe you're ready to put more in your own—or switch careers to something you can thrive at even more.

If you're jealous of their confidence, maybe work on how you present yourself.

If you wish you had their relationship, maybe it's a sign it's time to stop settling.

Envy isn't about them. It's about what *you* want more of in your own life.

### The Plan

For every insight, list one small action you can take today or this week to move the needle closer to what you want. Not a big ask. Just one action. Say yes to the date. Apply for that job. Cut the toxic ties. Start that passion project. Book the damn haircut.

This is about momentum, not instant change. One step leads to another, and soon, you'll see significant progress toward achieving the things you once envied in others.

PART II

# WHY YOU ARE
# WHO YOU ARE

# 7.

# What Are Your Roots?

## *And Why They Don't Define You*

Imagine you're making a docuseries or a podcast about yourself—like a true crime investigation into your history, piecing together clues and events from your past to find what might be holding you back. Take notes. Think back to home, school, friends, relatives—the whole picture of things that impacted you during your formative years.

Who were the biggest characters in your early life—in school, in your neighborhood, in your home? The heroes, the villains, the ones who made you feel seen, or the ones who made you feel invisible?

What were the biggest core rules you grew up with? The strongest values that could not be sacrificed?

What things did your family or community drill into you, whether they were helpful or not?

Hold on to your answers—these are going to be the props and players that will set your personal stage for this next section of the book: your roots.

When you're a little kid, you don't have much, if any, say in how your life starts. You're just a little sponge, soaking up whatever the world and adults model for you. Adults—presumably those who raised you—make the rules, set the boundaries, and create the environment that you learn to navigate, and over time, you learn to adapt to what is expected of you.

Growing up, I remember feeling like I was paddling against a current of other people's expectations of what was deemed "right"—who I was supposed to be, how I should act, what I should like and dislike—just trying to survive. But here's the thing: these early choices, the ones made by other people, can really stick. They stay with us longer than they should and shape how we see ourselves and the world.

It may seem obvious on the surface, but take a moment to really process this fact: *your early identity is almost entirely built on someone else's decisions.*

It's not just the small things, like that you were always dressed in blue because your sister got to have the color pink, how you were never allowed to cut your hair short, and were always given dolls to play with even though all you wanted was to build things with LEGOs. But it's also the deeper, unseen stuff, like how you behave, what you value, taste, and what you think you want or are supposed to like.

Whether consciously or unconsciously, the people who raised you made the rules. They decided what was acceptable, what was safe, and what was "right." Their choices were probably well-intentioned, arising out of a desire to protect you. They wanted to help you thrive.

But even well-intentioned decisions can leave deep wounds and emotional imprints that follow you into adulthood. You walk around with these old roots—things you might never have chosen but absorbed without question when you were impressionable and too young to know any differently.

Have you ever done something and immediately thought, *Why did I do that?* Maybe you impulsively said something you wish you hadn't, or acted in a certain way that didn't feel right.

Chances are, something you learned early in your life influenced that decision.

I remember being told I was always "the quiet one," the kid who didn't cause trouble and kept to himself. There I was, a shy little kid sitting in the back of the class, never raising my hand, but deep down, wondering why. Why couldn't I be the one who jumped up and shouted answers or made the whole room laugh?

I didn't consciously *choose* to be the shy one, but as soon as that label stuck, I internalized it and it became part of who I was. Whether true or not, it became a facet of my identity, a root that grounded me in a specific version of myself.

As a result, even when I tried to be more outgoing or adventurous, say something funny that popped into my head or get a little loud, a voice in my head always told me, *That's not who you are. That's not what people want from you.*

As I grew older, I began to realize that the voice wasn't mine. It was the voice of the people who told me I was the quiet one—my parents, my siblings, my primary school teacher, the peers who hadn't spent more than ten minutes with me outside of a structured classroom setting. That wasn't something I chose for myself; it was chosen for me.

For years, I lived with that root and let it define me. I clung to its familiarity and the implications it had in my life, even though it made me feel trapped. Maybe I even used it as an excuse sometimes. But once I started digging into the history of what kept me small, I could see the layers of expectation, shame, and limitation buried there underneath such a seemingly innocuous label.

As the quiet one, I was unable to say no, unable to stand up for myself, or set boundaries. I internalized a sense of shame. The quiet one label made me think that people assumed I would have nothing interesting to say, which is a demoralizing thought for a child.

Roots can either nurture you or shackle you. Sometimes they can choke the life out of you. This root was shackling me in my formative years growing up, but once I untangled myself from it—my real self—I could finally breathe and grow. It made me wonder what other roots needed untangling.

Your roots can often be cultural ones, too. As an Englishman, I have repression baked right into my core. It's a matter of national pride. "Chin up. Stiff upper lip." The saying "Keep calm and carry on"? That's not just a slogan, it's a deeply ingrained mindset. When you grow up in a place where keeping things inside and not showing emotion is the norm, breaking out feels like fighting against a tide.

I bet you have similar moments where you were assigned beliefs or personality features, told who you are, and what you should be by people you trust—even people who don't know you well. It's easy to absorb labels without questioning them, especially when you're young.

*You're not creative; you're good with numbers.*

*You're too serious; you can't take a joke.*

*You don't want to do that; it's not cool.*

*You're the responsible one, so don't mess up.*

*You're not as smart as your sister.*

*You don't look good in that color.*

As a kid, you don't have the tools yet to know your personal truth versus someone else's opinion. Imagine, for example, that you're a kid and an adult says, *"You don't have the right body to be a dancer."*

In the absence of certainty, you accept what you've been told, and then try to process it: *I don't know if it's true that my body is the wrong type to be a dancer, but I'm also not getting different feedback that contradicts what I've been told.*

How does that affect your feelings about your ability to become a dancer—or even other sports or activities? Or your feelings about your body? Or how you associate your potential?

The "Root Belief" is planted: *I shouldn't dance because I don't have the right body.*

Then that root is watered every time the belief is reinforced.

The "Growing Belief" becomes: *It's fine because I don't even like dancing, I'm not built for it, I'm not good at it, it makes me feel bad about myself, and I feel anxious and insecure anytime I'm anywhere there is dancing.*

Here's the seed that should have been planted: *Everyone can dance. Some will be better dancers than others. And those who dance the most and work hard to improve will probably be the best.* END. OF. STORY.

These labels and developed beliefs become the foundation through which you see yourself, strangling the real truth and your self-perception. It's hard to free yourself, especially if those labels and beliefs are reinforced repeatedly during our most vulnerable years.

What else has been planted for you? How much of who you are is actually who you chose to be? Is your education or career path your own decision or one you took because that's what was expected of you? Is the way you behave and see yourself rooted in your truth, or something handed to you when you were too young to say no?

## NOT SO GREAT EXPECTATIONS

It's a blurry line deciphering what you chose versus what you adopted. It reminds me of that legendary "Cerulean sweater speech" in *The Devil Wears Prada*, where Miranda Priestly explains how fashion is decided by couture designers' runway shows and in the editorials of fashion magazines, which dictates what trickles down to the masses, seeping into the collective consciousness without anyone really knowing.

In the same way, choices you thought you made of your own free will were often chosen for you SUBLIMINALLY! From the moment you were born, you have been influenced by everything and everyone around you. You followed the breadcrumbs laid for you obliviously, unknowingly compelled, compliant, and trusting.

It's hard to break free from external expectations, especially when they are ingrained so deeply that they're almost undetectable. And sometimes, it's just easier to lean into the version of you that others expect—the responsible one who plans the travel itineraries, or the middle child who always plays peacemaker—even if it doesn't feel right. In the face of someone else's perception of you, it takes bravery and assuredness to stand up and say, *No, that's not who I am.*

The reality is those expectations are so powerful. Many of us were taught that meeting them meant acceptance, and failing to meet them meant exclusion. As a kid, you'll do anything to be accepted. You'll mold yourself into whatever shape you want to get love, approval, and safety.

At the time, you don't know what will happen if you don't perform to the set expectations, but you're definitely afraid to find out. Will it change the way people feel about you? Will it change your standing in your family, school, community, or with friends? What, if any, freedom do you have to modify the expectation?

This concept doesn't even occur to us until we're much older.

Here's the kicker, though: What you're getting is not genuine acceptance. It's just a performance that must be continuously repeated to keep their approval.

It is so twisted when you look at it in retrospect, even if, to some degree, a little of it is unavoidable. The power of suggestion is undeniable. Sometimes, it's just one thing a person of influence has said: a teacher, a coach, an older sibling that stays with you forever and shapes everything. And in the end, you're robbed of the opportunity to figure out who you are because you believe what you were told.

## MY OWN ROOTS

I'm the middle child of five, raised in Leicester, England, by parents who endured unimaginable trauma in their childhoods. Mum and Dad did the best they could to raise us, but they had their scars.

My mum was just ten years old when she found out that her parents had been murdered. She and her sister read about it in the newspaper; that's how she learned about it. Can you imagine what that must have been like? She didn't even know where they were buried. Nothing. This was long before the internet or smartphones, so they were given no information and no way to get any more details.

My mum and her sister were placed in the home of an abusive relative. Mum spent the following years simply trying to survive until she could run away. This was at a time when children had no voice. They were to be seen and not heard. Their pain was not addressed, seen, or validated. Therapy and trauma processing were nonexistent.

My grandmother (my dad's mother) left the family when my dad was only five to start a new family with another man. In her absence, his father couldn't manage three kids alone, so he sent my dad and my uncle to live at a boys' home, a very rough orphanage. My aunt, meanwhile, was kept at home to do housework and cooking.

When I think about what my mum and dad endured, how traumatic their childhoods were, I am awed by their resilience.

My mum and dad escaped their abusive upbringings and found each other when they were just sixteen years old. They clung to each other, creating the kind of stability and normalcy neither had. We were poor and had little to call our own. While I never felt unloved, I always felt out of place.

I was aware from a very young age that I was wired differently. I didn't share the same interests as the other kids, including my siblings. My brothers liked football and the "typical boy stuff," while my sisters enjoyed the "typical girl stuff." And me? Even at home, I was the odd one cutting Barbie's hair. I felt disconnected—from my brothers and sisters, school, and world around me.

I had dyslexia, though it went undiagnosed and unrecognized. From a very young age, I was told by my teachers that I wasn't very good or intelligent. At school, I'd look at the board during lessons but didn't know what the teacher was talking about. I'd try to memorize what I could or write things down, but I felt lost and bewildered. I just couldn't understand; I didn't know where to begin to *try* to understand. The stuff on the board didn't mean anything.

How were the other kids doing it? How did this make sense to them and not to me? The teacher used to put red lines through my work; everything that I wrote incorrectly with the letters transposed, completely misread words, or mistakes made due to my confusion about the instructions, and my mum would get mad. She'd go into school, take on the teacher, and tell them, "You can't do that. It makes him feel stupid, and he's not."

I was bullied relentlessly and beaten up at school for being different. Eventually I was placed in what was then referred to as the special needs kids' class, where I didn't fit in and felt isolated.

There's so much more visibility about dyslexia now. It just wasn't properly recognized when I was a kid. People learn in different ways, and that's more understood now. Whereas when I was a kid, there was one way to learn; if you didn't learn that way, the assumption was that you were stupid or lazy.

There's one moment in my life that I always come back to: I was six years old, standing by my bedroom window, staring out at the gray, gloomy sky in Leicester, England. I remember the overwhelming sadness that struck me at that moment. I felt as colorless as the sky, unnoticed and invisible. I knew I was full of colors, but I felt trapped into someone bleak and lifeless. I felt I didn't belong where I was already.

That's what primary school felt like for me, and I thought leaving it would be a fresh start with new opportunities. Instead, it was the beginning of a nightmare. Upper school wasn't just harder academically, it was brutal socially.

I think that's the age when kids start to compare themselves, when they start to find their place in the hierarchy, and when they start pushing out anyone who doesn't fit into their mold. I didn't fit into a mold.

By age thirteen, I had found something I loved and seemed to have a talent for: hair. I got a job at a salon that I enjoyed. I didn't overthink it, because I loved having the ability to make people feel good. That love quickly became a weapon used against me.

Most of my friends at upper school were girls. They'd see me at the salon and think it was cool that I had a job and knew about hair. The lads, on the other hand, didn't like that at all: not only was I different, but I had fully embraced something they saw as feminine. The bullying escalated from occasional to relentless.

Every day, from the moment I stepped out of my house, I braced myself. The hour-and-a-half bus ride to school was torture. I'd sit, hoping to be left alone, but it never worked. The whispers would start, then the laughter. Someone would throw something at my head—a pencil, a ball of paper, food. If I ignored it, they'd take it further. A hand smacking the back of my head. My bag being yanked off my shoulder and thrown down the aisle.

And that was just the morning.

At school, there was nowhere to hide. In the corridors, I was shoved into walls. In class, people would whisper just loud enough for me to hear, calling me names and snickering like I was some joke. Gay. Freak. Faggot. At lunch, I'd sit with my girlfriend and her friends—they all thought it was ridiculous that I was being accused of being gay because I did hair. I tried pretending like the slurs didn't bother me, like I was untouchable. But deep down, it hurt.

One afternoon, walking home with my friends, two popular kids from school, the ones everyone in our class admired and who always got away with everything, were waiting there. Before I even knew what was happening, I felt a fist slam into the side of my head. They shoved me into a gate, kicked me, spat on me. And everyone just watched. Not one person stepped in.

I had never felt so small in my life.

I called my parents, and they went to the police. Instead of stopping, the bullying escalated. Now I wasn't just the kid who did hair, I was a snitch. The whispers turned to full-on taunts; the violence became more frequent. I couldn't walk down a corridor without my heart racing or my body tensing for the next hit, insult, or humiliation.

I stopped sleeping properly. My anxiety was constant. Even at home, I couldn't escape it. I'd replay everything over and over in my head. Why did they hate me so much? What had I done? I started believing that maybe I was the problem. Perhaps if I changed or hid the parts of me they didn't like, it would stop.

I started feeling trapped, like there was no escape, no matter where I went. School was hell. The bus was hell. Outside, I had to look over my shoulder, ready to defend myself constantly.

Eventually, I couldn't do it anymore. I stopped going to school. I'd wake up and get dressed like I was going, but instead, I'd go to the park and wander around town. I'd go anywhere but there. It was easier to be alone than to keep putting myself through the constant fear and humiliation.

But isolation has a way of getting to you.

The more I ran from school, the more I started running from myself. The world had told me, over and over again, that who I was was wrong. And I began to believe it.

I buried myself in my work. Hair was the one thing that made sense, the one thing I was good at. If I could just be the best and prove everyone wrong, maybe one day it wouldn't matter what they thought of me. Maybe one day, I wouldn't have to run anymore.

But at thirteen, that day felt impossibly far away.

And so, I kept running.

Hair became my escape, obsession, and way of carving out an identity that had nothing to do with my personal life back at school. It was a way to exist without having to answer the hard questions. It was a way to define myself beyond my roots and the target that seemed to always be on my back. It wouldn't be until much later in life where all this would start to catch up with me.


One of the biggest challenges to self-awareness is realizing that much of the baggage you carry *isn't even yours*. The limiting beliefs and fears you hold on to aren't truths, but are created by someone else long ago and projected onto you. You can't live your life constantly trying to meet everyone else's expectations, and you can't define yourself based on other people's labels.

Maybe there wasn't any negative messaging around those expectations, but simply the absence of positive messaging and reinforcement that did the damage. Either way, these beliefs grow roots in your mind, and the longer you carry them, the more difficult it becomes to differentiate between what's *you* and what's been forced upon you.

But here's the good news: there are new truths about who you genuinely are now and who you want to be moving forward, just waiting to be discovered.

You just have to start digging a bit deeper into the roots first.

# 8.

# Your Roots Are Showing

## *Whether You Want Them To or Not*

*How did I get here?*

*H*ow did I get here?
I've asked myself this question more times than I'd like to admit—both out of genuine curiosity and also feeling like a victim. Out of frustration, regret, confusion, and a heavy dose of anger to chase the disappointment down. I've felt like a kite caught in a hurricane, desperately holding on, waiting for the inevitable snap. In one especially challenging chapter of my life (more on that later), my world came crashing down completely.

The interesting twist is that while our roots are born out of decisions that we didn't make, now, as adults, our roots are nourished and grown by the decisions that we *do*.

Even with the best plans, and most solid intentions, you can still find yourself in the wrong situation that you walked right into. For me, it wasn't that I stumbled into these wrong situations; I ran straight toward them—willingly. I kept repeating the same patterns, sacrificing my own happiness to make others happy and avoiding conflict instead of having honest conversations. Getting tripped up by the same problems, overextending myself and then feeling resentful about it. Only to end up back on my ass again, head in hands. How did I end up here, again?

At some point, I understood that my perspective needed to shift. I was asking myself the wrong question. Instead of *"Why does this keep happening to me?"* I needed to be asking:

*"Am I the one doing this to myself?"*

When I asked myself that, the way my stomach sank told me it was true. Something was fundamentally wrong with how I was living. I wasn't simply stuck in some cycle of bad luck or poor timing—I was actively participating in it. My approach to life was the problem. I wasn't a victim of my circumstances.

Another hard question: *Was I doing something to keep attracting or creating these situations and unhealthy relationships? Or was it something about me?*

In my case, it turns out it was both.


How you are wired to act, react, and even what you attract into your life all stem from your roots. These core experiences of your formative years—whether idyllic or not—are everything, and you cannot escape their impact. We all carry the weight of wounds, criticisms, and judgments cast by the players in our life. Even the so-called "perfect" childhoods can still leave scars. Everyone is haunted and traumatized in some way.

The real question is, how does it affect your life now—how are your roots showing today in ways that you don't even realize? How are you actively keeping them alive?

To understand how your history influences your present— why you are the way you are, why you act the way you do, why you attract certain people, and why you sabotage your success— you must examine your roots.

Your past is like a constant echo that follows you around. You get so good at tuning it out because you've been hearing it for years. But what if instead of ignoring it, you started to listen to it closely? Really listen to what it's saying. You'll be surprised at the power it has. Trust me, the rotten roots can strangle the tallest trees.

I realized this when working my way up early in my career. I was evolving and having some success, finally booking bigger jobs and clients, but feeling utterly insecure and unworthy of it. Regardless of how hard I worked to earn them, I questioned my accomplishments and achievements and felt undeserving of my rewards. I was programmed by the opinions I had absorbed from others of what I could do or be.

Then, I actively made decisions and choices stemming from those opinions: I skated around the edges of intimacy, unable to embrace it and unwilling to be vulnerable with those who tried to love me. I kept a controlled distance because I feared that if I were seen and known, the things I despised about myself would be confirmed. The truth I was hiding, and the lie I had been living, would drive people away. If those who tried to love me knew the real me, they would run.

I couldn't accept love, or even my success, because I was so firmly planted in ideas of who I was based on decades-old assumptions.

But what I didn't realize then was that *roots can grow.* They are not cemented in stone for eternity, they can be replanted in new directions. Nourished. Revived.

Just like you can change your hair color to be more vibrant or better suit your face shape, you can change your root beliefs that have been holding you back. Your roots do not define you; you define you.

As a hairdresser, I should have connected those dots sooner, but I couldn't see the forest for the trees. Once I took a step back to investigate the deeper parts of myself—my history, my early experiences—I realized that's where the answer was hiding.

For years, I carried a quiet and heavy shame—the kind that sinks into your soul before you even realize it's there. I felt different. I continued to struggle with dyslexia, constantly falling behind in school, and never felt like I measured up to my brothers or the other boys around me. I felt broken and ashamed, almost like I missed the memo on how to be the kind of man the world seemed to expect.

So, what did I do? I hid.

I tried to suppress or hide the parts of myself that didn't align with how others saw me, hoping to blend in and avoid being singled out, teased, and bullied again. It was exhausting. For a long time, I truly believed I had to trade who I was for who I thought I *should* be. I was smothered by expectations and assumptions that were never mine, yet I was still the one carrying them.

The labels I was given as a child by my parents, my teachers, my peers, and my community or society at large—quiet, shy, unintelligent, not man enough, not good enough—were never who I truly was. It didn't fit me then or now. They were scripts forced upon me, but my truth is far more nuanced and complex.

But just because these beliefs have taken real estate in our mind for years doesn't mean we're stuck with them forever. The beauty of self-awareness is learning to let go of what isn't serving you. After some sincere self-reflecting, you can *choose* which beliefs about yourself are worth questioning and ultimately worth rejecting.

So let's get to the root of toxic, damaging beliefs and dismantle what isn't yours or doesn't reflect your true self. Doesn't that sound like the kind of change worth fighting for? Imagine what could happen. Imagine if you gave your kids or future generations the gift of not having to carry the same rotten branches and dead leaves from your own life.

## WHAT TO DO ABOUT IT ALL

The change you want isn't just about introspection—it's about action. Choosing to dig up your roots and pull out the weeds is how you strip the past of its power and begin healing. The ghosts can't haunt you if they're not your ghosts anymore.

Here's how we can start.

### Step One: Dig Up Your Roots

Reflect on the messages you absorbed growing up. Write them down if that helps. Sometimes things appear more real when you commit them to paper.

- How were you ever told "you're too . . ." or "you'll never be . . ."?
- How were you criticized for how you look, spoke, or thought? Did someone tell you that you couldn't pull off a particular look, didn't have the right body type, or weren't smart enough to achieve your dreams?
- As a child, were there moments when you felt unsupported or misunderstood? Was there one time you needed someone to get you or help you, but they didn't?
- What were you taught about yourself from your parents, teammates, teachers, friends, or even society? What labels were you given? Maybe they no longer resonate, or perhaps were never true at all. Check off any of these labels that were assigned to you at a young age:

| Foolish | Stupid | Messy | Clingy | Moody |
|---------|--------|-------|--------|-------|
| Cowardly | Too Shy | Predictable | Chaotic | Indecisive |
| Lazy | Pessimistic | Vain | Defensive | Insecure |
| Arrogant | Self-centered | Gullible | Clumsy | Quick-tempered |

**Step Two: Pull Out the Weeds**

Look closely at the beliefs you've just unearthed and consider the repercussions they've had in your life—these are all the weeds they've spread around your tree trunk.

- How do they impact your self-esteem, determine your actions, strain your relationships with family or friends? Influence how you show up in the world?
- What real truths about yourself do these beliefs block you from seeing?
- What do you still hear in your head today when you're doing something new or scary?

**Step Three: Get Rid of the Rot**

Here's a reality check: some of the roots in your life are toxic. Maybe they were planted for you, maybe you continued watering them, but either way, the toxins have spread through the tree, and they're killing you—holding you back, keeping you stuck in patterns of dysfunction, shame, and old behaviors. And if you're being honest with yourself, you *know* it. Those habits are choking the life out of your potential.

But the answer isn't just about adding *more* aspirations, new friends, or positive changes to your life; it's cutting away the toxic ones. Otherwise, you're just taping new leaves to a dead tree—and all that transformation you want is never going to stick.

You might think, *This sounds good, but how does this play out in real life?*

It plays out by severing ties with toxic people and setting boundaries in your dysfunctional relationships. You nurture the parts of your life that matter and cut away the things that pull you down. You let your past mistakes be the past, not something you're shackled to or defined by, and you create new conditions in which you can grow.

*It's never too late to cut the rot.*

So look at your family, community, important people, and impactful childhood events. What are the things you love that you've carried forward? What are the bad habits, negative behaviors, the shame and dysfunction that you have strapped to your chest like a time bomb?

Stepping away from it all will enable you to flourish. The process of growth and transformation is as much about *release* as it is about *embrace*.

I know from experience that it takes courage to cut the toxicity out, even if it feels like you're destroying a part of yourself. But trust me, your future is way more exciting than anything you left behind.

**Step Four: Plant New Seeds**

Now what do you do with the empty space that's left behind? It's time to plant better seeds that can root and bloom, even in less-than-ideal conditions you may find yourself in. Seeds that are hearty and can thrive because they feed off the strength of your character.

Envision the healthiest version of yourself—one where you aren't defined by other people's expectations or judgments.

Ask yourself: Who do I *want* to be, beyond these labels? How do I want to show up in the world? What must I believe about myself to move forward with confidence and freedom?


Repeat these questions and exercises every few weeks as your new roots start to grow. And remember, it's not about being perfect; it's about progress. Every time you pull up a weed or cut off a rotten root and replace it with something that nourishes you, you're one step closer to living as the person you're meant to be.

# 9.

# Your Roots Are Not
# Your Limitations

## *Even Though Everyone Loves
## an Excuse Not to Try*

When I was in my twenties, I was determined to build a name for myself and my hair styling portfolio. I was hungry for something bigger, trying to jump from salon to editorial, fashion, and celebrity clients. I would travel two hours by train from Leicester to London to work unpaid jobs. They were small, seemingly insignificant gigs for little magazines or advertisements for small local businesses, but I was happy to do them. I just wanted to get my work seen and recognized.

I was driven by the belief that every job was a step closer to my dream, no matter how small.

I took my portfolio to an agency that represented hair and makeup artists and they agreed to take me on. I felt like I was officially on my way. I was gaining momentum, my reputation thus far had been impeccable, and I was becoming confident that I was solidly on the ascent.

After a while, when I had proven myself to be a bookable talent who does excellent work, I met with my agents to discuss my next phase. It was time to aim higher and dream bigger. I told my agents that I always dreamed of styling for *Vogue*. For me, it was the peak—the ultimate achievement in fashion and hair. I wanted the people working with me, representing me, selling me as talent to know my ambition.

I remember the agents exchanging looks and politely laughing at me.

"You're a salon hairstylist from Leicester," they said. "You'll never do *Vogue*. You should think more about work that fits you."

*Work that fits me?*

Their response was, to say in the least, not what I expected. My agents, the people who were supposed to champion my career—who took a hefty fifteen percent cut of all my bookings—told me to stay in my lane. They told me to remember where I'm from, accept limitations based on my background not my talent or ability, and not get any crazy ideas about being more than that.

They didn't see me, and they didn't see the vision I had for myself.

I knew at that moment that I had to leave. I needed to find another agent who could see what I could become, not just where I came from. My agent then booked me a job doing hair for a commercial selling flip-flops. That was the level they saw me at, and that's when I realized how limited their perspective was.

I've done six *Vogue* covers and numerous editorial layouts for anyone counting, and I suspect there will be more to come.

It's sad when people, especially those supposed to support you, squash or put limits on your dreams. People tell us to stay in our lane based on where we come from, what we've done, or who we were told or expected to be because that's what they're comfortable with.

And maybe you even do this to yourself, stifling your growth by your own hand.

You internalize the idea that you can't be more than what people say, or you don't believe you deserve something more significant. But you do.

If you remember one thing from this book, let it be this:

~~~~~~~~~~~~

*You don't owe your past any*
*more of your future.*

~~~~~~~~~~~~

There's beauty in those early places, moments, battles, or events that have shaped who you are at a young age. But it's also important to remember that your roots don't determine how tall you grow, or in what direction you get to stretch. Your life can still be shaped, cut, and transformed. Your roots are a starting point, the place where your life grows from, not a final destination. They can ground you and remind you where you came from, but they don't have to limit you.

Maybe you grew up in a small town where everyone knows everyone else's business, but that doesn't mean you can't move to a bustling city where you can blend in anonymously. Maybe your parent never cooked, but that doesn't mean you're destined to a life of ordering takeout. Perhaps you grew up in a family of doctors and feel pressured to follow in their footsteps. That doesn't mean you can't pursue a life in the arts.

Life is an a la carte experience. You can take something and keep what you need and what serves you, leave the rest behind or burn it to the ground.

Don't set a ceiling on your own potential. Your experiences and background inform you, but you decide what you want and how to pursue it. Carrying emotional wounds from your upbringing can keep you *too* humble and have you thinking too small.

Whether you were told you're not smart enough, overheard you're not capable enough, assumed you're not good enough, or believed any of those things because there was proof at the time, doesn't mean that it's true now. These ideas about yourself become rocks in your shoes, and you wonder why you struggle to run the race—or why you always sit out.

The limits break when you realize that these beliefs are not truths but inaccurate assumptions, misunderstandings, or wounding words you were told.

While you look at the limitations you feel because of your roots, remember that these same roots made you more adaptable than you realize. You have a toolkit of emotional and practical tools you may not even know exist. All the experiences you had in your youth—being forced to take lessons, doing chores, or being denied whatever thing you so deeply wanted—those are the things that developed your critical thinking skills, endurance, and resilience, forging the neural pathways that serve you now. The core of who you are can serve as your compass, even if your identity is in complete reaction to or rebellion from your roots.

Limitations can be lies that we never questioned or discredited. Getting rid of those lies opens up the path in front of us and widens the road you get to travel.

## CHALLENGE AND REFRAME YOUR LIMITING BELIEFS

What are the things you still believe about yourself that trip you up? What negative thoughts or beliefs sneak in and make you second-guess who you are?

Think about the ones that show up when you're doing something important, like asking for something you want or trying to set a boundary.

For each belief, can you find evidence that DISPROVES this belief?

**Belief:** I don't think people really like me.

**Evidence:** I have a dog that freaks out (in a good way) every time I walk through the door. My coworkers still always sit by me at lunch when they could sit anywhere. The waiter at the sushi bar gave me extra attention and smiled way too much for it to be just part of his job.

With evidence, the story shifts.

Can you flip this old belief and rewrite it as a positive statement to reframe it accurately to represent who you are and who you are becoming?

**Old Belief:** I don't think people really like me.

**New Belief:** I know I am likeable because people go out of their way to engage with me in the office.

I know I am likeable because I was sent five memes yesterday, which means people were thinking of me.

I know I am likeable because I am a cheerleader for my friends, supportive of others, and fun to be around.

## PRACTICE A NEW LANGUAGE

Maybe you feel like it's easy to sit here, stare at these pages and engage with the lies about you out of context. But the practice of reframing them is not unlike learning a new language: you can stay at home and study the right vocab all you want, but the knowledge can vanish the moment that you're out in the real world. It takes practice to remember and reframe. The real challenge is catching those old beliefs when they pop up and then flipping them in real time when you need to.

What will you do when your old ways of thinking try to make a cameo? How will you nurture yourself and shut them down before they gain any ground?

What's your game plan when you feel an old belief starting to creep in? How will you show yourself love, compassion, and strength when it feels like the past is trying to drag you back?

This is when you show yourself that you *don't have to be stuck.* You can reframe, rewire, and do it in a way that feels right for you.

## THE LIE, THE LIMITATION, THE LIBERATION

When you consider the lies and limiting beliefs that you carry about yourself, after reframing them through the exercises above, then I want you ask yourself: What truth will liberate you from this false belief and the limiting thoughts that try to throw you off track?

Examples:

**The Lie:** Things are what they are. I feel fine about my life, who I am, and what I've done. (There's that *fine* word again!)

**The Limitation:** It feels like reflecting on my past isn't going to change anything or make it any different, so why bother?

**The Liberation:** I'm reading a book about personal transformation, so maybe I'm not as satisfied as I pretend to be. Reflection gives me context and a deeper understanding of myself and the events in my life. It's a better use of my brain and time than scrolling my phone mindlessly. Reflecting makes me realize that settling for "fine" keeps me from chasing "better."

**The Lie:** People like me don't become successful in the career field I want.

**The Limitation:** I didn't attend an elite school, so I have no opportunities. No one will take me seriously in the business.

**The Liberation:** Oprah Winfrey, Steve Jobs, Madonna, and Frank Lloyd Wright—all college dropouts. Some of the most successful people didn't follow traditional paths. Success is possible for anyone, including me.

**The Lie:** I should stick to what I know.

**The Limitation:** Playing it safe feels comfortable; why risk it?

**The Liberation:** Taking risks opens new possibilities. I won't regret trying something new; if it doesn't work out, I can try something else—and at least I'm closer to success than I was before I tried.

Your Turn:

**The Lie:** I've always been . . .

**The Limitation:**

**The Liberation:**

**The Lie:** I've never been good at . . .

**The Limitation:**

**The Liberation:**

## WHO ARE THE MIRRORS?

Remember in Part I how we walked through the ways we can fight the inner critic in our mirror? Now I want us to consider how other people can serve as our metaphorical mirrors.

To better understand the impact of our past, who you've been and who you've become, you can simply look around at the people in your life today. The friends, family members, and other members in your life act as your mirrors, showing you reflections of yourself that can help you recognize your strengths and weaknesses—sometimes in beautiful ways, sometimes in downright uncomfortable ways. You see yourself in others just as they see themselves in you.

I see myself in my own children, how they laugh and what they find funny, how they wring their hands when they're nervous, and how they approach the world with an unfiltered lens. I see myself in their stubbornness, their strengths, and yes, even in their flaws.

It's like looking into a mirror that reflects not just the past, but the present, the future, and every single version of me I've ever been. And it's not just my kids. I see myself in my parents, my siblings, my friends.

Those closest to you are often the ones who hold up the most accurate mirrors. They're the people who can reflect back the parts of you that you've been trying to hide for years. And it's the most viscerally felt when others reflect our flaws and insecurities that stem from our roots. We see and hate our worst parts in someone else. It's why family can be so triggering, and why some friends feel like they *get* you in ways no one else can.

They see it all—the good, the bad, and the messy parts you're not proud of and try to keep secret.

When you start getting honest about where you came from and where you're going, these people become the mirrors you can't escape. They hold up your heart, soul, trauma, actions, and sometimes your shame from your past.

And trust me, some of those reflections can be necessary to face—even as hard as it may be.

## MIRRORS AND LIMITS

To unpack the mirrors in your life ask yourself these questions:

*Who are the ones in your life who truly reflect you to yourself?*

Name the people who help you understand the most *accurate* and *transparent* picture of yourself.

How do they reflect your strengths? How do they reflect your flaws? Are there patterns in the way they see you?

*Who reflects the parts of you you've been avoiding?*

Think about the people who are the most challenging for you to be around. Do they make you feel uncomfortable? What do their reflections show you? What about their perception of you makes you squirm?

What does that tell you about what you need to face?

*Who in your life limits your growth?*

Some people are stuck in the past and simply don't want to create a box for you to change. Some people may not like the new version of you because it makes them question their own choices.

Who are they, and why are you still holding on to this relationship? Do you feel obligated to shrink for them?

Remember the mirror goes both ways, and not everyone will love the reflection they see in you. They'll try to project their stuff onto you, act like they don't see you, or critique you in ways that make you question who you are. That's their insecurity. It's not your job to deal with their discomfort or shrink yourself so that they feel better about their lack of growth.

In other cases, people may not even look at you so they can avoid that mirror altogether, or they won't engage because what they see in you is too much for them. Maybe you've made certain choices they wish they'd made, and your path illustrates their perceived shortcomings. Or perhaps it's because what you reflect back to them forces them to confront parts of themselves they've been avoiding.

Ever notice how people don't know what to do with someone living unapologetically? Or how people only want to see the version of you that they're comfortable with?

That's because the mirror they see in you is one they don't know how to face. You remind them of what they can't or won't see in themselves.

And honestly?

That's their problem, not yours.

You can choose which mirrors you face, and which ones you walk away from. You're writing your script, and how others see you doesn't define who you are. Keep reflecting, keep growing, don't be afraid of the mirrors that show you the truth.

Sometimes, that's precisely what you need to move forward.

# 10.

# Where the Growth Begins

*Untangling the Roots That Stunt and
Chopping the Ones That Strangle*

My childhood came with a set of instructions. It wasn't in a shiny manual or anything, but the message was loud and clear. When I was growing up, it felt like my entire life was drawn out for me—imprinted, etched, branded into my destiny by the place I was born, the family I belonged to, and the invisible lines that told me exactly where I could and couldn't go. Everything felt like it was set in stone.

The town I lived in, the house we called home, and how my family operated—it all felt like my life was being written for me. The expectations were clear, even if they were never explicitly said. There was a sense that if I stepped outside of those boundaries, didn't behave, didn't fall into line, or expressed myself as I truly felt, there would be consequences. So, I did as I was told. I stayed within the kind of lines that felt like safety, but also like a trap. Those around me told me who I should be. They told me what I should want. And most of all, they told me what was *possible* for me.

I thought that who I was then—based on where I came from—was who I would always be. Those roots, the story of my past, felt like the map to my future. I felt this sense of being tethered, like I would *always* be held in place.

Until somewhere along the way I realized—*Your roots don't have to be your noose.*

Yes, they hold history. But they are not meant to hold you captive.

As a child, I was brought up as a Jehovah's Witness. I didn't know any different. It was just the way things were. We went to meetings, listened to the teachings, and followed the rules we were taught. One of the strongest beliefs drilled into us was that giving blood was wrong. But even as a kid, I had questions. What if one of us were dying? Would you really let that happen? I never voiced my questions out loud, but the thoughts lingered.

The truth was, we never followed the religion to the letter. We still celebrated Christmas and birthdays even though that was supposedly forbidden. We were told blood transfusions were against God's will, but I knew that if I ever needed one, my mom wouldn't have hesitated to save me. That was the thing about faith in our household: it was there, but it wasn't absolute.

Looking back, I understand why my mom clung to it. The pain that comes from both of your parents getting murdered, that's the kind of loss that leaves a hole in a person that's almost impossible to fill. Religion, in a way, became a lifeline for her. It gave her something to hold on to when reality was too painful. A sense of hope. A promise that there was something greater beyond the suffering she had endured.

But by the time I was around ten, we stopped attending meetings altogether. I don't remember a big decision being made—religion just faded out of our lives. Still, I found myself praying sometimes, even though I wasn't sure who I was praying to. Was it God? Was it just the universe? Or was prayer a habit, something ingrained in me from childhood?

All I knew was that I wanted to be a good person. That's what I held on to, even when the structure of religion disappeared.

And maybe, in a way, that was my first taste of reinventing

myself—learning that I could find my own path toward the same goal. I didn't need to follow a set of rules to be good. I didn't have to keep playing the same part in the family play written for me as a kid. I could grow outward *from* my history, *without* being stuck or held back by it.

Once I started seeing my past as soil, something incredible happened. I saw possibilities for living my life according to my own beliefs and principles—and that life that once seemed so out of reach began to bloom.

The blossoms didn't just appear overnight, though. They slowly started to reveal themselves, like petals opening up everywhere, individually and all around me, as if they'd been waiting all along.

I realized that the instruction manual, blueprint, or map of my life I thought was carved in stone had been drawn in pencil all along. I really began to understand the reality of this—not just on an intellectual level, but on a soul level.

Your roots can anchor and ground you, but don't have to stop you from stretching toward the sun. A tree uses its roots to stabilize itself while it reaches up to the sky, higher than anyone could've thought possible. It doesn't stop growing just because its roots are buried "too deep" in the soil, too far down and too stuck to change.

Again, and I can't say this enough: roots are where growth begins, not where it ends.

I know that sounds obvious or overly dramatic. Still, when you've existed solely within the confines of what's admissible in your family or socially acceptable parameters, it feels like being thrown a life preserver. You're in the deep end, and suddenly you've got something to hold on to.

I started to see my past, the bullying I endured, the agents who didn't believe in me, the environment I adapted to, not as a weight tethering me down but as the foundation, the *soil*. And soil is fertile ground, ripe for movement and change. The same roots that you feel pulling you down can actually give you the freedom to stretch beyond your past expectations.

## GROWTH DOESN'T ALWAYS LOOK THE WAY IT "SHOULD"

If you want to grow and become more than the narrative you've been handed, you have to let go of those beliefs that have been implanted in you since childhood. Letting go of these inherited beliefs isn't easy. They feel familiar, like home. Like something you've carried with you for so long that it's hard to imagine life without it. Challenging them can feel like you're betraying everything you've known. You might even feel like you're turning your back on your family, community, or the foundation that shaped you.

*But here's the thing about growth:*
*it isn't about betraying your roots.*
*It's about expanding them.*

Progress doesn't follow some perfect linear path, and it can't be measured by anyone else's standards but your own. It's letting go to follow your curiosity, the quiet, internal voice whispering that we can live differently.

It's messy, it's experimental, and sometimes it's downright awkward. But that's where the magic is.

Trying things you thought you couldn't do is growth. Branching out into a new cuisine you've been avoiding because you don't like change—that's growth. Running that half marathon you thought was impossible is growth. Signing up to get your passport—even if you haven't booked that solo trip to Paris yet—is growth.

What if you try doing something and you hate it? At least you *know*. You tried. You grew. You learned about yourself in a way you never could have by staying in the box everyone else wanted to put you in.

Do you know what's even better than "being right" about who you thought you were? *Finding out what you really like* and who you really are, based on your *own* experiences—not on a presumption.

Not on your parents' opinion.

Not on your childhood's opinion.

Your *own*.

Growth allows you to live genuinely, even if it's messy. And finding a life that feels genuine for you is the ultimate freedom because it means you no longer need validation like you do oxygen to breathe.

Your ticket to that kind of life awaits you. You can let go of all that has bound you and make room for the person you're becoming.

## NURTURING THE HEALTHY ROOTS

You can't grow new roots without feeding the ones that are still strong. This is where self-love and self-care come in. It's not just about cutting out the toxic stuff; it's about investing in the stuff that will take you to the next level. You need to lean into what makes you feel good, strong, and authentic.

Take a minute to ask yourself: What roots are you nourishing right now? What do you spend your energy doing? What do you spend your voice talking about? Are you watering the things that will make you grow, or are you stuck on the things that keep you grounded in a place you don't want to be anymore?

If you've ever noticed your friends or family stepping up and calling you out to become a better person—or on the flip side, you notice *them* changing in a positive way because of something *you* did or said, you know exactly what healthy roots look like. These are the relationships you want to keep and spend your time and emotional resources investing in.

If you actively nurture the good roots, you will attract that positive energy.

So look at your life. What's growing? Who is expanding possibilities for you, encouraging you to have a big life? Who and what are keeping you alive, vibrant, and moving forward? Who's reflecting to you the things you need to hear, even if it stings a little?

Those are the roots that can determine how tall and strong you'll stand.

It's about making space for the new, healthier roots to take hold—the ones that support your dreams, desires, and future— not the ones that try to trap you in the past.

## WHAT YOU DON'T OWE

Remember that you don't owe anyone an explanation for your growth or an apology for changing, evolving, or stepping into your power.

I recently went to lunch with a friend whom I hadn't seen in almost a year. When she walked into the restaurant, I didn't recognize her at first because she had completely changed her look. I was looking for her, someone with dark wavy shoulder-length hair, and she had cut all her hair off, shaved the sides, and dyed it a soft lavender. She was Megan Rapinoe's doppelganger. She also had gotten nearly a dozen small fine needle tattoos on her arms.

When she approached my table, my jaw dropped, not in shock but in delight. Before I could say anything, she rushed to say, "I know, it's different. You hate it."

"Hate it? Are you kidding? I LOVE it!" I hugged her. "When did this happen, how did this happen, and where have you been hiding this side of you?"

"I think I've always wanted to be more edgy, but everyone knows me as being so straitlaced and serious. Turns out, the real me has tiny tattoos and purple hair."

She seemed happier than I remembered her ever being, and I remember being so bummed that she felt like I wouldn't approve of her choices. It made me think of all the times I've apologized for changing or evolving beyond who I was.

The truth is, the people in your life will either support your growth or resist it. Either way, it's not your responsibility to make them feel comfortable. Your responsibility is to be true to yourself, honor your path, and keep moving forward, even when the mirrors around you start to crack.

Unfortunately, that means sometimes you must let go of relationships that no longer want to reflect your truth. It's okay to walk away from people who can't support the new version of you. *It doesn't mean they're bad people.* It just means that your growth isn't always going to fit into the boxes other people have created for you.

When those mirrors start reflecting things you don't want to see, remember this: You don't owe anyone the reasons behind your growth. You don't owe them your truth. What you owe is yourself the freedom to be who you are—and to keep moving forward.

## WHAT YOU DO OWE

The most important things you owe are to yourself. Above all, you owe yourself the right to evolve, and you owe yourself your advocacy. You owe yourself your utmost effort and care to make your life better when a "better" exists.

Consider the people you just identified in the above section who bring positive growth to your life. The ones you want to invest in. You can owe *those people* your best self and your best effort. If you mess up or hurt someone, you can owe them change. Take responsibility for how you impact others rather than excusing yourself from that duty.

You do owe others something. Namely, the respect of honesty and communication. Your growth isn't a free pass to leave a trail of destruction behind you.

Relationships are complex, and the changes you make in your life have a ripple effect—especially for the ones who have been with you on your journey for a long time. Some people deserve a seat at the table and an opportunity to adjust to your growth, while others do not.

# 11.

# Life in the Shadows Is
# Never Your Best Option

### *How to Really Let Go of the*
### *Shame, Guilt, and Secrets*

There's more to why you are the way you are. Some of it is the stuff that you probably never speak about—your shame and guilt. I know. It's heavy. Even just writing the word *shame* used to make my body tense up. I remember carrying the burden of mine with me every waking second for so many years. I'll share my story with you in the next chapter, but I want to talk about these big crippling issues first.

I'm sure you know that feeling, whether simmering at the surface or deep inside. It's a discomfort at best and a gaping darkness at worst. Even if your shame and guilt have no consequences or repercussions for anything anymore, you can't seem to rid yourself of the bad feelings. Why? Because your shame and guilt feel like they're a part of you. Like they're *yours* the way a scar is.

As uncomfortable and painful as these emotions are, they've become part of your normal state of being. You probably don't know what life feels like without their familiar weight. Your shame and guilt continue to shape your choices. They built the walls you hide behind and the defenses you use to protect yourself. They can keep you feeling afraid of connection. They can steel you toward the world, angry at everyone in it.

By pulling them out of the shadows and into the light, you diffuse their power.

It's human nature to want to keep certain parts of yourself private. We've all got things we're not ready to share. But there's a difference between protecting your privacy and letting your shadows and secrets imprison you.

*Do you really want to dedicate more of your life to hiding the truth than living it?*

I didn't.

You can't forget or deny the things and events that shaped you, and you can't keep shoving these feelings down, hoping they will disappear. The only way to unclench their hold on you is to try to understand what it is. You need to look at your shame and guilt not with fear or denial, but with a forgiving curiosity.

## THE ROOTS OF SHAME AND GUILT

**Shame** is not something you're born with. It's something that grows inside you like an infection. Slowly creeping in during your childhood in little moments that might not seem like anything really, but which were very influential. They were those times when you were reprimanded for something you didn't fully understand, didn't know any better, or know how to do well. It was the disappointed look from a parent or a sharp, offhand remark from a teacher or a friend. It was every time you felt different or misunderstood. You have shame for your private thoughts and desires, and even shame offloaded to you by others that has become your own.

There are a thousand ways it happens. Shame gets its claws in early and tells you that you can't escape your past—you're tied to it forever. And that's a lie.

Shame and guilt are cousins, but they aren't the same. **Guilt** is connected to *action*. You feel bad about something you did or didn't do. You're haunted for a moment when you were cowardly or cruel, dishonest or hurtful, or when you did harm. It's the lies you told, the wrongs you've done. The nagging feeling follows you around like a mistake you need to make right.

Rounding out these big baddies are the secrets. **Secrets** are like little seeds planted in the dark corners of your mind, growing roots you don't even see. Many of them are intertwined with your shame. You learn to keep quiet about things you've done, that were done to you, or that you were party to. Things so potent that revealing them would alter how you're viewed by those who matter most.

You learn to keep quiet about things that hurt you. The things you don't want to admit to yourself, much less aloud to others. The things you feel too embarrassed to talk about because you think you'll be judged or that no one will understand.

Your shame, guilt, and secrets don't have to be nightmare fuel. You can dig up those roots and get rid of them—but first you have to expose them for what they are.

## WHY YOU BURY YOUR SHADOWS

You bury guilt, shame, and secrets because it's easier than facing them head-on. It's exhausting to unpack all that and feel those feelings. Who wants to go through so much pain?

But buried feelings don't vanish. They come out sideways.

Maybe it shows up in the form of a bad habit, like biting

your nails or drinking too much. Maybe it's a pattern of self-sabotage, like always being late to work or keeping the people you love waiting. Maybe it manifests in your relationship with your body, hair, or appearance. Maybe it's even in how you show up for people—or how you don't or can't. Guilt and shame are sneaky little bitches. If you don't confront them, they control you in ways you don't even realize.

It's time to look around and survey the damage done by the lies you tell yourself. They're preventing you from achieving real intimacy with those closest to you, and ultimately dictate the choices you make to keep them buried.

*Your mistakes don't have to be your roots.* You're not the bad decisions you've made, the things you regret, or the parts of your past you wish to erase.

## LETTING GO IS NOT ABOUT LOSS

For me, when I hear the words *letting go*, my mind immediately goes to some kind of loss. Maybe it's a person, a relationship, a job, or an old version of myself. It got me thinking about how letting go is framed as a sad, sorrowful act you only do when forced, not a choice you make from a place of confidence.

But letting go doesn't have to be a loss. *Especially* when what you're releasing is connected to your shame and guilt. When you let go, suddenly, there's all this space to be filled with new and better things. It's like cutting off huge portions of damaged hair or cleaning out a closet so cramped that you can't even see what's hidden. Everything becomes clearer, fresher, and feels better.

*The real power of letting go*
*is rooted in possibility.*

That's where you need to shift your mindset. It's easy to hold on to things in your life because you're comfortable with the discomfort. It's a devil you know, a pain you know you can manage, and maybe have even become weirdly attached to. But I promise you, the safety and consistency of the shadows is never a better place to be than the light, even when it's unfamiliar or scary.

What's in front of you is *far more important* than what you're leaving behind. The best isn't behind you—it's still ahead of you, waiting for you to make space for it.

I recently told one of my clients this very thing. As the saying goes, there's a reason the windshield is larger than the rearview mirror—it's because you're meant to keep your gaze forward, only glancing back to where you were when it helps you keep moving ahead safely.

Once, my client had been obsessing over an ex who had already moved on with a new partner, even though their relationship was incredibly toxic. He said that maybe if he had been more agreeable or easier to be with, if he had committed to the relationship earlier or more fully, if he had gone to his partner's sister's wedding in Italy even though he couldn't afford it, or agreed to get a dog together, they would still be together. It was just a slew of "what ifs" without the "what actually was" parts.

I reminded him that the relationship ended because it needed to. They brought out the worst in each other and behaved terribly to one another. Why would he want that back or want to be that version of himself again? Didn't he remember how unhappy he was in that relationship?

"You're your worst to the people you love the most. That's what a relationship is," he muttered, flipping through his ex's Instagram.

"Where did you learn that?" I asked.

"That's how my parents were to each other and my brother and me."

"That sounds like a painful way to express or receive love," I said gently. "Have you considered the idea that you're confusing acts or proclamations of love as an apology for shameful behavior? Because it sounds like there's a cycle to break here."

Holding on to shame and pain will only keep you prisoner to the rearview. You'll never stop looking back. And that's no way to live.

## EVERYONE HAS IT

Letting go doesn't have to be a big cinematic event in your life, either. Most people don't think about "letting go" as a constant process of small everyday moments. It's little daily ways to push away the embarrassing moments that haunt you; to resist the daggers or backhanded compliments from a friend, to shake off the indignities that are thrown your way.

I've worked with incredibly beautiful, talented, and successful people whose biggest private challenges have been plastered across every visible medium. And I've watched them have to make a career of "letting go"—of the mean comments, the horrible headlines, the constant invasion of privacy.

Personal moments of public-facing people are constantly documented and misrepresented for entertainment clickbait, not just by the paparazzi but by anyone with a smartphone. Years of constant public scrutiny and criticism about every choice of how they look, how they live, who they date, love, or leave, how they behave, how they build their empires, and do their business. It's impossible to ignore, even for the most insulated people.

Many celebrities have been incredibly open about the struggles they face and the mental health toll of the constant public shaming online, from strangers and the media. They've spoken about the weight of being in the crosshairs of popular opinion and the incessant crowd-sourcing effort to guilt and shame them about every facet of their life, from people who have zero regard for the trauma they're inflicting or compounding on them or their families.

I've been in the trenches with them when they've been taunted by reporters or paparazzi yelling at them about their personal lives, looking for a reaction to spin into more misery as fodder. It's pain on top of pain.

Yet I've seen firsthand how these powerful and possessed women have found ways to confront the pain rather than give into it. They inspect it closely, process it, and use it as fuel to fearlessly stand out instead of shrink. They turn that shame into strength, proof they can withstand, survive, and rise above. They are unapologetically themselves. There is a lesson in that for everyone. Your shame can be a springboard instead of a sinkhole.

## IMAGINE YOUR LIFE WITHOUT GUILT

*Ask yourself:* What if you let go of the hold that memory has on you? What would you do differently without it? If you didn't feel so afraid to bring your shame, guilt, or secrecy into the light?

Imagine what life would look like without that baggage. What new choices could you make?

When you think about your past choices, what do you wish you had done differently for each instance?

Now what would you do if you could start over?

*Exercise:* Write yourself a letter about the things you've been holding on to that make you feel ashamed. Maybe you ghosted a friend. Maybe you cheated on a partner. Maybe you failed at your dream job. Whatever it is, get it all out. No filter. Try to capture the size and shape of these things that haunt you.

Now shred it, rip it up, set it on fire.

It may sound silly, but it's a symbolic release. You can start over—every day.

This isn't about blame or making excuses. It's about understanding that those moments don't define you and don't look the same as they did when they happened. You are not the sum of your mistakes. You are not your secrets. You are not your shame. You are evolving.

## IT'S ABOUT THE FREEDOM

Once you've trained your mind to let things go, you'll probably start to notice something: the past doesn't have the power over you that you thought it did. It loses its grip. You don't have to forget what happened, but you *can* put it down now. That was just a part of who you once were, and now it's time to let that part evolve into something else.

You will feel a very real shift when you finally get a grip on the roots of your shame, guilt, and secrets. You will start making different and better choices. You will start showing up for yourself in a healthy and compassionate way you might never have before. You will let go of the need to prove anything to anyone anymore. You will feel a freedom you haven't felt in years—maybe ever.

It's not about wiping away your shame, guilt, and secrets with a magic eraser. It's about acknowledging the trauma and telling yourself, *This happened, I've examined it, I understand it, and it doesn't have control over me anymore.* You can walk away from it with your head high, knowing that your past doesn't define you. It's just a rest stop on a drive that's not over yet—and each day you keep driving, it'll keep getting smaller and smaller.

You are a story of growth and redemption.

You can take mistakes that others would bury and use them as stepping stones.

You are not your deepest secrets and shames.

You don't need anyone's approval to grow.

You don't owe anyone your every flaw, mistake, or detail of your inner life.

Only *you* need to decide what moments are worth carrying with you on your back—no one else gets to determine what you keep.

You don't have to be shackled to your fear—starting today.

# 12.

# Rising from the Roots

*How I Destroyed My Life to Finally Live It*

I wanted to write this book because I have lived and had to work my way through some serious life-altering shit. I wrestled with my roots, my shame, my guilt, and my secrets for so many years that it seemed impossible that I would ever find happiness, feel contentment, or live my truth without injuring those I love most.

I was in my late twenties when I began the process of coming out. For me, this wasn't just about telling the world I was gay. It was about letting go of the version of myself I had built. It was about accepting that the life I had constructed—the one I thought was keeping me safe—was also holding me back, and walking away from that was the hardest thing I've ever had to do.

Change means loss. Even when you know you're heading toward something better, you still grieve the life you're leaving behind. As you're about to see in my own story, I wasn't just losing a relationship, a home, or the illusion of who people thought I was—I was losing the security of the familiar. And no matter how painful that familiar life had been, it was still mine. Letting go of it felt like losing a piece of myself.

I'll be honest; initially, I felt like I was falling apart and unraveling piece by piece with no idea how to put myself back together. Should I go back or push through? I genuinely didn't know what I was capable of. But with each new step that I walked into my new life, the more I realized something: I wasn't breaking. I was rebuilding. And that felt exhilarating in a way I had never felt.

You will feel this way, too, when you get there.

When you finally embrace who you are, it's life-changing. Not just in how the world sees you but in how you see yourself. The shame that once felt unbearable starts to fade. The guilt that weighed you down starts to lift. And for the first time, you breathe like never before—with your whole chest, your whole body, your whole mind.

Change isn't just about becoming someone new. It's about finding your way back to who you were always meant to be.

And yes, it's terrifying. It's painful. It will shake you to your core. But on the other side of that fear, uncertainty, and loss—there's freedom and peace.

Picture this truth: there is a version of you that isn't just surviving anymore. There is a new version that is finally living.

I spent years fearing change. Now I know it's the only reason I'm still here.

## THE PATH

I didn't officially come out until I was twenty-seven, after living a straight life for years—girlfriend, two kids, the whole picture. And when I did, it wasn't just about saying "I'm gay"—it was about dismantling the version of myself I had built for everyone else and starting over.

By this time, I was already more successful than anyone would have deemed probable. Everyone knew who I was and where I came from, both in my town and in the industry in which I was making a name for myself. I wasn't under the radar anymore. I knew I had a great life: a family, a house, and a job doing what I loved, one that allowed me to create beauty and transformation through hair. I could show people a version of themselves they hadn't thought possible. That was my superpower.

All of this came after I had barely survived my childhood and young adulthood. I had lived a version of myself that felt safer and fit into the world's expectations for me. I molded myself into a shape that would be acceptable, morphing for any given set of people or circumstances, taking my lumps along the way, which were plentiful, to put it politely. I learned to hide the unrelenting anxiety and distress I felt daily.

Looking back, I started hiding long before realizing that's what I was doing.

While my brothers and the other lads were playing football, I was learning to cut my mum's and sister's hair and experimenting with hairdryers, curlers, and hot tools. In school, I was seeking refuge from the relentless torment of the boys who said I was gay before I understood what being gay meant.

I remember when my mum sat me down and explained what she knew. It was not much, as society was still relatively un-educated at the time, and there was tremendous fear and dire consequences associated with homosexuality. She told me that being gay is when two men get together, and there's this thing called AIDS, which makes you sick and die.

Can you imagine? Die? I didn't want to die, I didn't want to hurt my mum and dad, so I didn't want to be gay. This was all before I was old enough to have even a real interest in anyone, much less a sexual orientation that I was aware of.

When the boys at school found out I started working at a sa-lon, things got worse. There was nowhere to hide from the daily taunting and violence. I didn't just deny any accusations of being gay constantly hurled at me; I set out to prove them wrong. I told myself that if I could live a "normal" life and be what they expected, maybe I could erase the doubt in their mind. Perhaps

I would be safe. I didn't understand it. I was only thirteen, had always had girlfriends, and never been attracted to boys before. It was all puzzling and exhausting.

At eighteen, I began a relationship with my coworker Kate, and by nineteen, my son, Billy, was born and I became a father, which further cemented me into a heteronormative life that I was building for myself. And it felt right.

Everything was moving in the right direction. A couple of years later, we had our second child, Kitty-Blu, a house, and my hairstyling reputation and career were rising. At twenty-six, I won the Young Hairdresser of the Year competition and was styling some of England's most famous models and stars. I had a beautiful life that, on the outside, looked exactly the way it was supposed to.

Yet nearly nine years into my relationship with Kate, things were breaking down and we were growing apart. My work was taking me away from home more frequently as my job expanded. There was a lot of traveling abroad, a lot of events, drinking, and going out. Being outside of Leicester, there was a freedom to explore outside of the confines of where I was from. In London especially, where I was spending a lot of time, there were artsy people, there were cool people, there were gay and lesbian people—it was a city, it was different than living in a small village where less was acceptable.

One time when I was away for work, I met someone interesting. At the end of the night, we were both drunk, and he kissed me. I was surprised, but didn't think anything of it. It wasn't a big deal. I didn't tell Kate or anyone about it.

Then, when I got back to my hotel room, I was scared. I remembered my mum's words. Soon, I found myself in the bathroom brushing my teeth and tongue obsessively.

He and I exchanged numbers and began a friendship. We just talked; we were essentially pen pals. He lived in a different country, and I was still living with Kate and the kids, so it wasn't romantic, but I was confused by the feelings I had for him. We just got on really well and talked all the time. We're we just friends or was I developing a crush?

One day, he rang me and said he wanted to talk to me about something. I knew what he was going to say before he said it, but the words still hit.

"I need to tell you that I'm HIV positive."

Instantly, the walls came down. I went back to being ten years old with my mum telling me that's what happens when you're gay, you get HIV. That's the punishment for being gay. How ironic that the first gay friend that I developed an emotional attachment to now had HIV. I suddenly became convinced that I had AIDS, even though we had only had that drunken kiss and never any sexual relations. I got tested and retested multiple times. Even though I didn't have HIV or AIDS, I felt sure I was going to be punished even for the baby step of exploring any developing feelings for another man. It was a slap in the face that made me completely withdraw.

He told me he wanted to come and see me. I told him no. He came to England anyway and asked me to meet him, but I couldn't. My mind just kept looping. Being gay was a bad thing. It was a curse. I didn't answer the phone when he rang me, and I didn't see him again.

I told myself to stay on the path I was already on. I was just having some sort of quarter-life crisis. That this was just a random experience that happened. Maybe I was just looking for an out to my relationship with Kate. I was probably just exploring, and if I kept my life as it was, things would be okay. I could control this. The part of me that was questioning would eventually disappear. For a time, that worked.

## THE BLOWOUT

Six months later, I met someone in London. When we kissed, I felt something completely different. I couldn't deny my attraction to this man, nor could I vanquish it. We started seeing each other romantically when I went to the city, then I would return home to Kate, the kids, and my real life.

I wasn't sure if it meant that I was bi or that I was gay. I just wanted to be me and not be labeled. I was so sick of being labeled. Baby steps was all I could manage because there was still a part of me that believed that being gay was wrong. The constant tightness in my chest, the sinking dread in my stomach, and worrisome thoughts kept me awake at night. I didn't know how to make it all vanish.

But the truth doesn't disappear. It lingers. It waits.

No matter how much I tried to push it down, I knew, deep inside, that I wasn't living fully or the way I should be. I was making myself smaller, quieter, more acceptable again. I was shrinking into a life that I knew wasn't mine because I was too afraid to step into the one that was.

The cost would be too steep. In order to have the freedom to explore what I had been most afraid of, I would have to destroy our family unit and Billy and Kitty-Blu's stability.

Would the outcome of my destruction be worth it? What kind of person does that to the people they love the most? How could I live with myself?

Believe me, I tried not to. Coming out was the last thing I wanted for myself—until, day by day, it became the only thing I needed.

There would never be a right time for this. There was no good month, day,, or season to implode my life. To change my relationships with everyone who mattered to me and admit that I was not who I led them to believe I was. There was no window or perfectly timed moment that would spare my loved ones from the collateral damage.

I knew there would be talk. My kids would be teased at school and whispered about by their teachers or other parents. People would look at Kate and my family with pity, like they should've known. I'd be hated.

That's what I thought every second of every day.

Admitting to Kate that I was gay was awful, but the shame of keeping it a secret had become unbearable. I don't even re-member the words I said or what happened next. It was like I blacked out; my voice turned to static in my ears, my field of vision went blurry, and time collapsed.

We kept it from the kids and everyone else for a long time, because we honestly didn't know how to navigate it or what it meant for our life together. We were part of a community and an industry. Everyone knew who I was. They knew Kate and me together as a couple. They knew our kids. They knew our home. They knew our life.

During this time, I tried to detach. I saw myself as two sepa-rate people. To me, being gay was a cancer inside my body that I so desperately needed to cut out. I could keep my head above water in the daytime, but I was no match for the nights. I would have recurring nightmares about ruining the lives of everyone I love. I used to go to bed with a picture of Billy and Kitty-Blu clutched to my heart, praying that God, the universe, or some higher power or source would help me. I didn't want to hurt the people I loved. I didn't want to ruin all our lives.

Anytime people suspect there's a secret, the gossip and spec-ulation begin. Those who thought they knew me suddenly all had questions. They wanted explanations, clarity, reassurance—things I wasn't even sure I could give myself. It was clear that I would be outed soon if I didn't do it myself.

Kate and I decided we needed to tell the kids.


## THE BOTTOM

The one thing you want to do as a father is to protect your chil-dren from any pain, not to be the one inflicting it. I was terrified that they would have to endure the bullying, the name-calling, and the "being different" label that I had when I was growing up, and so desperately wanted to escape.

As I write this, my chest still tightens because I remember the fear I felt that night. Telling my kids was the most challenging and darkest moment of my life.

My biggest fear wasn't losing friends, family, or even the life I had built—it was the possibility that my kids would suffer because of me. That they would face the same relentless bullying I had endured, that they would be ashamed of their father. I wanted them to have a regular dad. A dad who wasn't whispered about, questioned, or judged, but that wasn't the dad they had. And no matter how much I wished I could be, I couldn't change that.

Kate, her mom, and I sat down with the kids. Billy was ten, and Kitty-Blu was eight. I still couldn't say the words "I'm gay" aloud. Kate and I were already crying before anything was said, and then Kate's mom blurted it out.

There was confusion and tears as Billy and Kitty-Blu tried to process what they were being told. My son asked, "Does that mean you're gonna hold your hand like this?" He held his wrist bent effeminately because this was what he thought gay looked like. My daughter just cried. She said she wanted me to be okay, but what she probably wanted was for this to not be happening. For me to just go back to being her dad. They both had questions that I didn't have answers to.

After I told them, I went into overdrive. It felt like I had just walked away from the man I had been for twenty-seven years, but I wasn't fully ready to embrace the man I was becoming: a gay man. That word, *gay*, still felt foreign, like a costume I hadn't learned how to wear. The shame and guilt still consumed me—guilt for hurting my family, guilt for being pulled into the darkness that I had been programmed to think being gay meant, guilt for being the thing I had spent my whole life not wanting to be.

That night, it all became too much. The weight of my guilt was unbearable. I convinced myself that it would be easier for my kids to say their dad had died than to say he was gay. That the world would be kinder to them if I just disappeared.

I was at rock bottom. I drove for hours, trying to run away from the pain of the mess I had made. I needed to get far away from the people I loved. To take this cancer of being gay away from my family.

I stopped at a liquor store I bought a bottle of gin. I checked into a hotel, downed painkillers by the handful, and drank the whole bottle. It felt like I was killing the part of me that I had spent my entire life not recognizing. The part that I hid once I realized it was always there. The part I blamed for everything that was falling apart. I called Kate one last time. My voice was shaking as I said, "I love you and the kids. I'm sorry."

The next thing I remember is the crash of a door being busted open. Strangers pouring into a room. The blinding lights. Being taken out on a stretcher into the ambulance. Kate had tracked my phone, figured out where I was staying, and called emergency services. She saved my life.

Miraculously, I woke up in a hospital bed, drifting in and out of consciousness. A couple of days later when the fog started to lift and I could finally think clearly, another wave of shame hit me like a tidal wave. I hadn't even succeeded at ending my life. And then, I felt more shame that I had even tried to end my life in the first place, which made me hate myself even more.

But then, something shifted. It wasn't in some miraculous, magical movie-moment kind of way. It happened quietly. Gently.

I was overwhelmed with a feeling I hadn't expected: gratitude. I was still here.

And even though I didn't know what would come next, and I still felt lost in the weight of it all, the register had changed. Because if I was still here, then maybe—just maybe—I wasn't meant to disappear. Perhaps I was meant to find a way to exist, even in discomfort.

I distinctly remember lying there and just . . . surrendering. There was a peace to it. I couldn't hate myself anymore. I couldn't fight myself. As importantly, my secret couldn't be used as a weapon anymore. You're right. I'm gay. What of it? What now?

Once you surrender to your truth, the whispers stop and everything changes.

I decided that my life was restarting now, and it was going to be a revelation.

## THE REBOUND

I know the idea that you can bounce back from complete annihilation, from making a disaster of your life, feels like an impossibility when you're on your hands and knees in the thick of the pain.

And that's precisely where I was.

How do you even start the process of starting over? How do you rebuild from the ashes of the inferno you started (or were thrown into)? How do you reinvent yourself into the person you want or finally allow yourself to be?

On day one, the only thing I could think of to do was to make a list—a short list. That was the bandwidth I was dealing with.

Instead of concentrating on the wreckage, I focused on getting out of the rubble. My Morning After Rock Bottom list looked like this:

What do I have?

1. The love of my kids, family, and friends (hopefully).
2. A career with potential and a strong portfolio to build on.

3. The opportunity I've been waiting for and the chance to start over.

## What do I need?

1. A new co-parenting arrangement that works for all of us.
2. A routine that keeps my kids grounded.
3. A flat to live in.

## What can I do?

1. Give myself grace.
2. Invest in my growth and fine-tune my ambitions.
3. Become who I am, without fear.

## What is out of my control?

1. What others think of me.
2. Everything besides my actions.

I don't want you to get where I was when I hit rock bottom, but I want you to know that if you do, you can rebuild. I want you to get to where I am now. I am being my true self. I am living the life I was meant to live, which is better than I could have ever imagined. When I keep doing the work, my life gets better, and so will yours.

I'm fifteen-plus years from when I made this list. My relationship with Kate is stronger than ever, she is still my best friend. My kids are happy and thriving, and my career has taken off in ways I couldn't have dreamed of when I first made that list.

From the bottom of my heart, I want to tell you that if I can do it, so can you.

# PART III

## WHO YOU CAN BE

# 13.

# It's Time to Get Unstuck

## *And to Start Failing Your Way Toward Success*

Have you ever felt trapped? Constrained by the way you see yourself, or maybe how the world sees you? It's as if no matter how much you've grown, people still define you based on who you used to be. It's frustrating. To try and be more than your past, yet still shackled to it.

But you are not a fixed thing: you are in a state of constant development. There is an incredible kind of freedom in realizing this, that you can change how the world sees you. Not by pretending to be someone you're not, but by manifesting and then stepping into who you truly are now. A version that maybe you've been too afraid to show before.

Reinvention is all about revealing the strength, confidence, and potential that's inside you through vulnerability and self-awareness. It isn't just the clothes you wear or how you style your hair—though those things matter—it's about your unique energy that only you bring into the world.

How many times have you wanted to be seen differently? To walk into a room and have people notice that something has changed, that something about you has shifted?

I've seen through my own clients that a person who's been overlooked can often be the very person who becomes someone impossible to ignore. A once timid person can step forward with quiet but undeniable confidence. A person who was once dismissed can command respect. All of this is within your power by standing fully in who you're meant to be.

But first, you have to get unstuck.

This is the time to decide who you want to be and what you want your life to look like, but more importantly, what you want to *feel* like moving forward from this moment.

Not too long ago, I found myself with a spontaneous client. She wasn't the kind of person who needed attention. In fact, she made an art of staying just out of the frame—close enough to influence everything, but far enough that the spotlight never found her directly. Kim's manager was sharp, calculated, and composed—the ultimate behind-the-scenes force. While Kim was making headlines, she was in the background moving the chess pieces, one decisive move at a time. You knew instantly when she entered a room—not because of noise or drama, but because of presence. Poise.

And her hair matched that energy perfectly. Long. One length. Dark. Immaculately maintained, but never indulgent. It was clean, safe, and above all—controlled.

She had worn it like that for over a decade.

No face-framing. No layers. No trends. Not even a subtle flick of volume. Just sleek, center-parted, straight-down-the-middle predictability. It was an image that said: *Don't look at me, look at my work.*

And that was the thing. It *was* always the same.

Sound familiar? Many people find a hairstyle and stick with it for most of their lives. They reach a certain point and stop experimenting. They assume they've found what works for them, so why mess with it? But being stuck isn't always as good for you as it may feel.

I remember the first time we talked about her hair—really talked. We were in the glam room, the kind of late night where you lose track of time, eating cold snacks in between outfit changes and touch-ups. She was scrolling through something on her phone when she casually mentioned how she hated how flat her face looked on camera sometimes. "It's just how I'm built," she shrugged. "I don't have cheekbones like Kim. I need the hair to soften things."

That line stuck with me—not just because of what she said, but because of how she said it. Like she'd quietly accepted a limit she didn't even know she'd set for herself. She believed she had figured out a version that looked "good enough" and stuck with it, like dulled armor. Somewhere along the way, she had stopped being curious. She'd mistaken comfort for satisfaction.

But I could see what she didn't. Her hair wasn't doing her any favors. It was masking her face, not complementing it. It was heavy, all one length, dragging her features down instead of lifting them up. It gave the illusion that her jawline wasn't defined, when in fact, it was. It made her look more tired than she was, more severe than she felt.

One day, I asked her a question—not out loud, but with a look. I held the comb in my hand and tilted my head just slightly.

"What if . . . ?" I started.

She looked at me and smirked, half amused, half terrified. "Are you going to change my life?"

"I'm going to give you what you give everyone else: your best." I pressed: "I'm not talking about change for the sake of change. I'm talking about change that excites you and gets your heart pumping and your energy shifting. Aren't you curious to see what else there is?"

She laughed, but then sat back and handed over her trust.

I started with the cut. First, I lifted the weight. Took off about three inches—not enough to scare her, but enough to give the rest of the hair room to move. Then I carved internal layers through the front, starting just below her cheekbones and blending down through the collarbone. These weren't trendy, choppy layers—they were sculpted. Intentional. I call it hair contouring—cutting with the same philosophy as makeup contour. Creating depth and light, softness and structure.

As I cut, I watched her eyes in the mirror. At first, skeptical. Then curious. Then silent. That's when I knew we had something. It was as though she hadn't considered change through the lens of *possibility* rather than fear.

I moved on to the color. Her brunette was beautiful, but flat—like a single note played on a piano. I added a subtle dimension with hand-painted ribbons in a neutral mocha tone. Just enough to catch the light and reflect warmth onto her skin. Around her face, I feathered in micro-lights so thin they were nearly invisible—but when she turned her head, they shimmered just enough to make her look lit from within.

When it was time for the blow-dry, I didn't say much. I let the cut speak for itself. Her face began to change as the hair dried. Her cheekbones lifted visually. Her jaw looked tighter. Her eyes looked brighter, like she had just returned from a long vacation and finally slept.

She didn't look "different." She looked *awake.*

She stood up from the chair and studied herself in the mirror. Tucked the front behind one ear. Flipped the part. Looked from the side. Then back again.

"I didn't know I could look like this," she said quietly. And then: "I actually feel . . . pretty."

That moment? That's what it's all about.

Over the next few weeks, I saw her start to experiment. She began showing up in front of the camera more, doing panels, interviews, even popping up on socials in ways she never used to. She wore her hair tucked, flipped, waved, or pulled back. She had options now.

The cut grew out beautifully. The way I'd layered intentionally meant that as it grew, it maintained structure. The contouring effect lingered for months, subtly flattering her face without demanding styling every day. The mocha tones faded like a sunset—never brassy, just soft and seamless.

That hairstyle changed not only her appearance, but also altered her energy and boosted her sense of identity.

She was taking up space in her own life again. The wildest part was that she hadn't even noticed how absent she'd been.

I get it. It's easy to stay stuck in your old habits and look. I see this all the time; it's an epidemic. You stay with things that don't suit you or aren't making you feel great simply because you're comfortable with the status quo.

Why?

*Because you can't know*
*what you don't know.*

Maybe you have no idea what else to pick. You're not sure what else you'll like, and change feels overwhelming. So you pick what you already do know, like keeping your hair the same way, even if it isn't doing you any favors. There is a safety to familiarity.

But we know that our comfort zones are not where the magic happens—growth lives in the discomfort.

The unknown doesn't have to be scary or big. When you're metaphorically standing in a room of doors and you're not sure which one to open, try reframing those doors as opportunities instead of seeing them in your mind only as *safe* or *unsafe*. Not knowing which door to open first doesn't mean you shouldn't open any.

Getting unstuck from the familiar is the first step. So, how do you learn to get comfortable with the uncomfortable? How do you break patterns that you've always chalked up to just being part of your everyday life?

You do that by understanding that *change is your friend*.

Being on the precipice of something new can be a thrilling place to be. Making a visible change is often the first step toward the edge. Step by step, the momentum picks up, and what may have felt scary can become thrilling.

Think of how you feel when sitting in the chair at the hair salon, ready for that cut or a new color you've been considering or obsessing about. Your body thrums in anticipation for the transformation you know is about to happen with that first snip or painted stroke of color.

I get that same buzz from the other side, being the one to transform my clients into a new version of themselves. Creating a safe environment for crossing the threshold between anxiety and anticipation is one of my favorite things to witness.

Part of why I wanted to write this book is because that threshold exists everywhere—not just in the hair salon.

We know from chapter eleven that we are wired to see ourselves in others, which also means we naturally can empathize with their triumphs. It's why you feel invested or moved when you read about a fictional character or total stranger reshaping their life. That visceral feeling is like a full-body fist pump, a jolt of complete YES! You feel it when the underdog gets the win. When the brokenhearted find new love. When the tortured walk away from the tormenter. You feel it when the need for change is finally met with the action.

And if you feel those feelings of relief and hope so deeply for others—why not feel it for yourself for once?

You have to get unstuck from an unsatisfied life and find something better. If you find yourself trapped in the same day again and again, and a whisper comes from deep inside saying, *there's got to be more to this* . . . You should listen. That voice is right.

## STOP CHASING PERFECTION

For you, maybe your problem isn't that you're stuck in the comfort zone—maybe it's that you're stuck in your pursuit of perfection, doing everything you can to avoid failing.

Admitting you need change is not a failure. It's freedom.

Even if you work hard to get your circumstances right, they can still be wrong for you. All of that energy you put into that job you thought would define you, that relationship you believed would save you, or that perfect persona you've curated for yourself—those things can all improve, but in a broader sense, they can still be the things that keep you stuck.

Embracing change does not mean you are or have been wrong all along. It just means you're evolving and examining things from a new perspective.

So how do you admit you need to change when everything about it feels like you're tearing up a part of who you are?

Have a dialogue with yourself. You might be scared to change something because you're terrified of being wrong. But let me get this out in the open—*being wrong is not the end of the world.* Being wrong is one of the most important steps toward being right—and maybe you can't even get there without being wrong first. I know it sounds counterintuitive. But think about it: How would you ever grow if you never made a mistake? You wouldn't.

Maybe you've changed your mind about a relationship in your life. Maybe you've tried a hundred different outfits before landing on the perfect look. Maybe you've painted over your walls a dozen times before finding the right shade.

Those moments weren't a million little failures; they were a million steps toward arriving at the right place. You saw things in a new light. You allowed yourself to be open to something else, something better, and you evolved as a result.

And meanwhile, other people around you are failing all the time, too. It's easy to look at someone else's transformation and think, *But they had it easier. They had more confidence, more talent, more strength than I do.* Guess what? They're human, just like you, and like you, they, too, were afraid of being wrong.

The difference is they didn't let that fear paralyze them. They're failing their way toward success.

When you look at the careers of some of the biggest celebrities, remember *they've all been wrong at some point.* Who hasn't been? Whether it was taking a role they hated for a big payday, staying in a toxic relationship, or following the wrong career path. Missteps and misfires are all part of the journey.

There is no such thing as perfect or perfection. Everyone blows it. That's just life. But the quest for either is often at the expense of *progress.* Perfectionism convinces you to keep pushing and work harder, but progress urges you to rethink your approach or shift altogether. Practice makes progress, not perfection.


I'll tell you about another client, a huge celebrity, someone you'd recognize immediately. I happened to be working with her for a beauty campaign when she was at a crossroads in her career. She'd been embodying the same perfect "look" for years: sleek, polished, flawless. The public loved it—it was what probably got her the campaign we were there to shoot. But privately, she felt alienated from herself. She had spent all this time building this image, but somewhere along the way, it wasn't hers anymore.

She confided in me that afternoon, *"I'm done with this. I'm bored being stuck in this thing I thought I wanted."* I thought she was experiencing typical burnout. The more we talked, it became clear: she wasn't just tired, she was *trapped* by the very thing that had made her famous. The constant pressure to be the polished, shiny, perfect version of herself when she felt like she was slowly suffocating.

The funny thing about being stuck in perfection is that it *looks* impressive from the outside, but feels like a pressure cooker from the inside. I told her, "You've built this beautiful image and I think it's time to shake it up."

She was immediately game and ready for the shift. She and I plotted, and after some discussion, I took her three shades darker and cut her hair in a way she never thought she'd go: messy, textured, edgy, and laid-back, a cut that showed off her personality.

In the end, this was a change that reconnected her with who she was, not the version of herself she thought she had to be stuck with.

Of course, she had to fight the pressure from her team, the media, the fans, everyone begging her to "go back to what works." But she didn't go back, and her career flourished in an unexpected way after that. She started getting noticed by directors and producers for roles that she wouldn't have been considered for prior. These new roles brought her more recognition than anything before. She was happier, more artistically challenged, and free—and she was most certainly not perfect.

Over time, I've found that wisdom isn't knowing the right answers. It's knowing when to admit that you're wrong, when you need to *change*—and then doing something about it.

After that, something amazing happens: you start to see possibilities. The world opens up, and you realize that *you* get to decide what happens next. Not your boss, not your partner, and definitely not society's expectations—no one but you is in the driver's seat.

What if this is just the beginning?

Making much-needed change doesn't have to be this dramatic, world-shattering moment. You might not know exactly what the next step looks like, but that's okay. Don't overthink it. Just ask yourself: *What would make me feel different?*

Maybe, it's a small, quiet, simple step like taking a break from social media to recenter yourself. Or maybe you've been staying too long in a city that you hate, and it's time to explore a new place that sets your soul on fire (or at least doesn't make you want to scream into a pillow every morning). Or maybe you need to step away from a relationship that's just not giving you what you need anymore.

You just need to get out of autopilot and start making your own moves. When you step out of your comfort zone and trust that life will catch you, even if you trip, the best things will start to happen.

# 14.

# What Are Your Real Intentions?

*Using Your Internal GPS to Level Up*

I t sounds dramatic, but I remember her like watching a sunset in a time lapse—imperceptible at first but then stunning in full bloom. That's the kind of impact her transformation had. It was cinematic, which is fitting, because I met her when I was styling a client—who happened to be her boss—for a movie premiere.

She had been running around, putting out fires, solving problems for hours. Sorting out premiere tickets and seating for VIPs, tracking down a missing clutch for the stylist, being pulled in a million directions by a million loose ends that needed tying as time ran out. She had a calm, almost detached energy about her, though the demands upon her as my client's personal assistant were chaotic.

Her hair was long, unstyled, and loose—nothing too messy, nothing too perfect. It was the kind of hair that told the story of someone just reacting to life as it happened to her. She moved through it without *participating* from her own point of view because she was accustomed to being of service to others.

At first glance, there was nothing wrong with it. Her hair looked fine, just like her life looked fine. When my client left for the red carpet and she had a moment of peace, I asked her if she wanted me to quickly do something with her hair before she went back on the clock. She had been hustling so hard, I wanted her to feel a little glam herself.

"Really?" She was shocked to be asked. "That's so nice. I don't usually do anything with it."

She sat in my chair, and we talked a bit while I combed through her hair, added some big barrel curls, and used some products to bring out some shine. Afterward, she couldn't believe how her hair looked and was so grateful that I would take the time. I gave her my number and told her to call me, and I would really happily do her hair again.

When she came to my studio, she was excited but shy about being there. She wasn't asking for anything big and didn't need any drastic changes—just "whatever I had time for."

I told her, "I invited you here. I have time."

As I ran my fingers through her hair, I had this feeling: she was hiding behind something. It was as if she didn't think about making any statement at all—like if her hair was just in a perpetual state of "fine," then she wouldn't have to acknowledge anything bigger that was missing.

She told me her usual hair story, how she had always "just let it grow out" and "never really bothered with it much. It's easy this way," she said, shrugging.

I understand the appeal of simplicity. But something about her voice—the way she said it—made me realize that it wasn't simplicity she was after. It was a lack of commitment. A lack of . . . direction.

"Can I ask you something?" I said, as I started to section her hair. "When's the last time you really *wanted* something?"

She looked up at me in the mirror, a little confused. "What do you mean?"

"I mean, when's the last time you said, 'I want this,' and *went for it*—with intention? Not just taking care of someone else's wants."

There was a pause. I could see her thinking, but I could tell she wasn't sure how to answer.

"I guess I've always just gone with the flow, let things happen. Been okay with whatever comes my way, and it's worked out pretty well. I mean, it's not my dream to put my degree toward ordering holistic dog treats and making sure there's the right kind of sparkling water in the production offices," she said slowly, like she was weighing the words as they came out.

"I get that. But here's the thing—life will keep giving you what you *accept*, whether it's what you want or not. It's the same with your hair. You've been letting it grow out without any intention, and now it's just . . . here."

She looked down at her hair, and for the first time, I saw a flicker of curiosity in her eyes.

"I never thought about it like that," she said quietly.

I smiled. "Let's change that. Let's set an intention for how you want to look and then make it happen."

After discussing and showing her some photos of hair that would flatter her natural canvas, I went to work. I started by cutting off the length—nothing flashy, but enough to make a noticeable difference. I added layers, but not just for texture. I cut in a way that gave her hair volume where it had previously fallen flat. I used my scissors to create space, to allow her hair to breathe and move. There was a purpose to each snip and layer.

As I worked, I could see her beginning to shift in the chair. She wasn't just a passive observer anymore. She was present, engaged in the process, and aware of each choice we were making together.

Then, I moved to the color. Her hair was a flat, dull brown—nothing wrong with it, but it had no spark. I mixed a soft caramel balayage, just enough to lift her face and warm up the natural tones. For me, these decisions weren't about following trends; they were about making sure every detail of her hair had intention.

The transformation wasn't about the final look. It was about the shift inside of her as we talked more about what she does want to do with her degree and want she does want her life to look like. She began to realize what it meant to make choices—not just let them happen to her.

When I finished, she didn't speak at first. Her eyes moved slowly from her hair to her face, and she laughed.

"I look hot."

"And how do you feel?" I asked, knowing the answer before she said it.

"I feel great. Different," she said, her voice filled with not surprise, exactly, but maybe wonder. "It's not just the hair. It feels like I made a choice, to come here and shake things up—and it paid off."

I smiled. "It feels good, right? To think about something long enough to be clear about what you want. That's living with intention. Your new hair reflects that."

She sat there for a long moment, running her fingers through the new layers, the soft caramel ribbons catching the light. Then, she looked at me and smiled—a real smile this time, not the polite smile she had when she first sat down.

"I think I've been afraid to want things because my whole job is focused on other people," she said quietly. "Or maybe I've been waiting for someone to tell me it's okay to *want* things."

"Well, consider it said. It's more than okay to want things. You're supposed to want things. It's *your life.*"

She left the salon that day with her hair looking amazing, but more than that, she left with a new mindset. What other choices—big and small—could she be owning, instead of letting the current just take her through them?

This is important: intentions are EVERYTHING.

Living intentionally will change your life exponentially for the better. I say that to you with my hand over my heart, swearing it as truth. Living intentionally is like unlocking your superpower. It's like suddenly having X-ray vision and being able to see what you couldn't before.

But what does living with intention mean, exactly? It sounds like a silly mantra or vague buzz phrase that you can't quite put your finger on.

To put it simply, your intentions are your objectives and goals. Setting intentions and living intentionally is to harness your aspirations, ambitions, and desires and let those inform your choices. It's like having an internal copilot that keeps you on your greater path.

Instead of drifting through each day as a passive observer, reacting to what happens, you're the one calling the shots. Once you start making active choices, everything shifts—your confidence, your happiness, your sense of self.

The difference between those who do and those who *wish* is intention and action. When you sit back wishing, you are essentially waiting for someone or something to come fix your problem. It's easy to cruise along in your default settings of *not doing*, but you won't get the life you want. You get it from conscious choice.

We've all gotten lost before, and probably will again. That's part of life. It's unavoidable and one of the ways we learn and grow as people. There's no shame or fault in being human. But there's also no need to stay lost.

Now it's time for you to get found.


You've spent parts one and two of this book considering who you are and contemplating the why of it by examining your roots. That's the heavy work. The bulldozer that clears your path to walk toward the life you want. You've taken an honest look at where you are right now—if its where you hoped you would be; if you're missing or wanting something; what parts of your life are in need of improvement or need an entire makeover.

In any given moment, you probably have this whole internal file where you shove everything you don't want to deal with. Your relationship with exercise, food, or that person in your life who makes you feel terrible about yourself. It's where your procrastination lives next to your un-updated résumé, though you secretly want a new job.

I'm not judging. I have one, too. I've just gotten better about cleaning it out.

Transformation, both internal and external, starts with intention. Start with what's working in your life. What is going fabulously? Where are the areas in which you excel and thrive? What are you most proud of? THAT is the level you want to live your life, so it's good to start by identifying the best parts and the feelings you associate with them.

It helps if you write it down and see it. Take a personal inventory of everything. This is only about clarity, and it's only for you. Be honest and specific, because a vague inventory is as useless as a phone without a charger.

Now consider the bad. And this part is not the time for rose-colored glasses or giving yourself a pass because of what you've been through.

What's NOT working? Is it your career? Your friendships? Your health? Your mindset? Your relationship with money? Your romantic relationship? Is it your style? Your haircut? Your wardrobe? Your attitude?

Then consider: How do you *want* those things to change?

Saying, "I want a better career," is a wish that will fade into the ether with those forgotten resolutions you made on

New Year's Eve. Instead, break that desire down into something specific, like, "I want to move from sales into a more creative department, or a job where I can use my writing skills."

Now you have something you can work toward.

When you set intentions, they should be laser focused and *actionable*. If you know what you want, SPECIFICALLY, you give yourself a clear target—and targets are for hitting. Then you aim for the bull's-eye.

The next big question is: WHAT IS BLOCKING YOU?

What's standing in the way of your transformation when it comes to that thing you're thinking about, besides life in general? If you want an excuse for anything, you can easily find one. I know I always can, time being my favorite one. So why are you procrastinating? Why do you keep talking yourself out of that next step you know you want to take? Is it fear? A lack of confidence? The fact that Netflix is a seductive siren pulling you into its abyss of "just one more episode," or you can't claw your way out of the social media vortex?

Recognizing what's blocking you is central to removing those blocks. Obvious, yes, but that file of things you stuff away is full of the obvious. Maybe old habits, past failures, or self-doubt keep you stuck. Whatever it is, it's time to own it.

Of course, there are concrete obstacles sometimes standing in our way. Maybe you tell yourself you need to wait to find a new job until you can save up and afford to pay off your mortgage. But we can still work with those barriers. Maybe finding a new job doesn't mean quitting and losing your salary as the first step—maybe it means networking once a week with someone new from the industry in the meantime. What's holding you back emotionally can also fuel your transformation if you learn to work with it.

I want you to remember this:

*Self-sabotage is the villain in
the story of transformation.*

Once you identify the villain, you can start to dismantle its power.

If you have self-doubt, break your barrier into small, manageable pieces that you can take on little by little. You might not be able to change your entire look today. That takes time and a possible trial-and-error period. So start small. Do your nails, buy an electric toothbrush, start a skin regimen, and build out from there. Sometimes, little accomplishments give you the confidence and momentum to take on more significant tasks. Suddenly, your self-doubt is replaced by proof that you can do complex things.

You've got everything you need to make your transformation happen. All you have to do is set your intentions and align your actions with what you've set out to do.

## THE THREE-ENERGY PLAN

I, personally, need structure or I'll get off course. The "Three-Energy Plan" is what helps me organize my intentions so that they are clear and actionable.

1. **Energy In:** What will you add to your life to move toward your goal?

This could be learning, taking action, self-care, or anything that fuels your personal growth. For example, if you aim to improve your physical health, you might add thirty minutes of daily exercise or make more conscious food choices.

2. **Energy Out:** What will you let *go of* to create space for your new intention?

This is just as important. Maybe bad habits, self-limiting beliefs, or toxic relationships are draining you. If you want to grow, sometimes you need to make room for it first.

3. **Energy Toward:** What will you focus on to make your transformation happen?

This is your North Star, your guiding light. Get excited about your goals. Feed your passion for it, think about it, talk about it with others. Align your energy toward it every day, even if it's just for five minutes. Get specific, get strategic, and get going. You won't regret it.

Transformation is a journey and every step, no matter how small, is progress. Give yourself some love whenever you take an action that aligns with your intention, even if it's just sending that email or going for a walk. Celebrate your wins!

What happens if you fall off the wagon? We all do it. Don't sweat it. No one is wagging their finger and tsk-tsking you. You shrug it off and get back on track.

Remember what we said in the last chapter—you aren't striving for perfection; you're making progress. Progress is allowed a cheat day.

Setting intentions isn't just about wishing for change. It's about knowing where you are, knowing where you want to go, and doing the work to get there. Transformations don't happen by accident but with clarity and focus, aka living intentionally, and some good old-fashioned hustle. When you align all of these things, you will become the things you once only envied.

# 15.

# Do You Need a Trim or a Chop?

*Deciding What to Keep, Toss, and Shape*

There are seasons in life that feel conducive to making changes. Maybe you're starting a new job, exiting a toxic relationship, empty nesting, or moving to a new city. You're on the edge of a new chapter and feeling inspired to ride the wave of momentum. It's as if everything you've been putting off is finally at the front of the line.

The question arises: *Do I need a trim or a chop?*

This is a dilemma transcending hair: it's a question of control, reinvention, and where you are emotionally. It's about reclaiming a part of yourself that feels stuck, lost, or restless. Sometimes, it's the battle between your inner self and what you wish you could *cut away* from your lives.

Have you ever noticed that after you cut your hair, it looks visibly healthier, fuller, and has more body? Even though you have less of it? That's because the health of your hair follicles has been improved, and you can tell. The change is measurable. Your hair is healthier, so it feels and looks better.

Cutting your hair can allow it to grow longer than not cutting it, as contradictory as it sounds. You remove split ends, dead ends, and damaged parts, taking off the thinned, frayed ends and leaving the healthy parts in their place.

When you don't cut off the damage, the strands of your hair are weakened. In other words, the damage doesn't *stay contained.*

It spreads, causing further breakage and making the hair prone to splitting further up its length.

Cutting off the damage = healthy growth

Leaving the damage = deterioration

That applies to everything in your life.
*What feels like less will actually bring you more.*
And when you don't remove or eliminate the damaged parts of your life, they contaminate the healthy parts. Toxic relationships, stressful environments, bad habits, compromising positions, and inattention to self-care, among other things, all contribute to the decline of overall wellness.

There have been countless times when someone comes to me for a quick clean-up and completely changes their mind. They'll be in my chair just wanting me to take a little off the ends and maybe add a few face-framing layers, and then once I'm cutting, they keep asking me to take off more. It happens all the time.

The excitement grows when you are in the midst of change and start to see a new possibility. There's a hint of the result, and the hesitation leaves your body. It's like doors permanently shut and locked suddenly swing wide open, and all you want is to run through them. An adrenaline rush happens because you can already see yourself differently.

What was meant to be one inch becomes seven, and the old stories and outgrown ideas lie on the floor waiting to be swept away.

A client once came in on a Tuesday between dropping off her three kids at school and heading to work. Her eyes were tired, but there was something else there that she wasn't letting herself fully acknowledge.

She sat down with that familiar smile, the one that says, *I'm fine, everything's fine and under control . . .* even when it's obvious that nothing is.

"What are we doing today?" I asked as I pulled the cape around her and released her hair from the elastic that held it all back.

"I just want something easy," she said, "You know, a trim. I end up wearing it in a ponytail all day anyway."

I nodded, noticing the way she held her body when she said it. Ever since she became a mother, I'd noticed this particular client always looked down when she talked about herself, almost as if her own needs and identity had literally fallen down in her list of priorities.

As I started to section her hair, I asked her about the school play she had told me about last time, the fundraising campaign she was heading for the nonprofit she was involved with, if her husband was still traveling for work, and how life in general was going.

"I'm just tired," she admitted, a small crack in her voice. "There's always too much to do." She laughed, but it wasn't a laugh that felt *light*. It was a laugh that felt like it was trying to make something feel better. "I used to care about my hair, or maybe I just had time for it. But now, it's just one more thing."

I paused as the gravity of that hit me. She had let everything else take precedence—her children, her job, her family—and in the process, she was quietly disappearing.

I took a step back. "Let's chop it off. Give you a chic pixie cut. Something that will look great with your face shape and grow out cool and messy. Very low maintenance, high style."

She raised an eyebrow, but there was curiosity behind it. "You think I can pull that off?"

"Absolutely. And I also think it's time to stop making your hair just something to 'deal with' when it could be something that makes you feel stylish and cool."

She agreed, and instead of a trim, I began cutting length and contouring her shorter hair into a sophisticated, sexy, playful pixie, layering and giving texture. This cut would give her something to move through easily as it grew over the next year.

She was quiet as I worked, but her posture had started to change—she was sitting a little taller now, a little more present, a little more like her own energy was coming to the surface.

When I finished, I ran my fingers through her hair, showing her the versatility of her pixie cut. I could see her face before she saw her reflection. There was a softness in her eyes and face. Suddenly, she seemed brighter, renewed, with a sense of clarity.

She touched the ends of her hair slowly, as if she were reacquainting herself with a part of her that had been buried for too long, as she looked at herself in the mirror.

"I didn't realize how much I missed this," she said quietly. "I feel cool again. I look really fucking cool."

As with many others, including my own mum going back to the early days when I used to do her hair in our bathroom, her haircut wasn't about saving herself time on her busy to-do lists—it was about restoring her identity as a person, not just a mother, wife, or professional.

Her life had become about serving others, but by making the chop, her light was coming through again. The next time I saw her when she spoke, it wasn't just about everyone else—it was about *her*. She'd made room for herself again.

I understand your resistance to change. I acknowledge your desire to dance with the devil you know, even if it's somewhere on the spectrum between boring and horrible. But as discussed in Part I of this book, you will no longer settle for the four-letter F-word. *Fine* doesn't cut it for getting the life you want.

So . . . are you ready for a trim or a chop?

Which parts of your hair and life do you want to preserve, which need to be removed, and which need refinement? This isn't about making a hasty purge or rash decisions. I'm asking you to be thoughtful about what will bring out the best version of yourself.

## THE TRIM

The trim is a safe zone. It's like dipping your toe into the pool's deep end without fully committing to getting wet . . . or swimming laps. The magic of a trim is that it's a measured risk.

You're taking control and taking action, but don't have to worry about drastic consequences. You feel like you're making progress without fully committing to a total overhaul. Something about trimming your hair feels akin to tidying up your life, which I love for my clients when it's the right time and place for it.

A trim is like putting a fresh coat of paint on your walls. It's rejuvenating and fills you with new optimism while still in the comfort of familiar territory. You're *fresh and polished* without straying too far from what feels safe. I say start with a trim and go from there when in doubt.

These Life Trims are subtle, but they'll make all the difference:

**Relationships with Potential:** Not every relationship needs a complete overhaul, some just need a little nurturing, attention, or a recalibration. These are friendships you want to hold on to that could flourish with more consistency and communication. With a little refinement, these relationships could become even more meaningful and fulfilling.

**Habits that Could Use Fine-Tuning:** Perhaps your routine needs a few minor tweaks. Instead of overhauling your entire morning, maybe all it takes is replacing that extra cup of coffee with water, stepping outside to put your feet in the grass at lunch, or introducing a brief meditation practice to start the day with clarity. It's in these seemingly minor shifts that real transformation begins to take root. Consider what habits could shine brighter with slight refinement.

**Clutter—Physical and Mental:** A clean, minimalist space is not just a luxury. It's a reflection of a clearer mind. Look around. Is there physical clutter in your life? What about digital clutter? (Unsubscribing from email lists is just as satisfying as decluttering your closet, trust me.) The same goes for mental clutter. What thoughts, habits, or tasks are you clinging to purely out of habit? This is your moment to simplify and create space for what truly matters.

## THE CHOP

The most daunting part of any big change is the act of elimination. Transformation can only happen when you eliminate the old, outdated parts of your life that don't align with the person you're becoming and the goals you have for yourself.

The chop is the big *decision*. When you cut your hair off, it's not just a haircut—it's a statement. It's a loud "I'm here for the change" moment. A chop feels like letting go of something heavy. It's the emotional release, an emotional breakthrough, and a physical rebrand all wrapped into one.

The chop feels like breaking up with an old version of yourself. This is the change you dream about at 3:00 a.m. deep into a life crisis. The chop is the haircut equivalent of slamming the door behind you on your way out.

There's no going back once you decide, which is a big part of the appeal. It's a clean slate. You're shedding whatever weight has held you back and starting over. The chop is messy, wild, and unpredictable but also *freeing*. It's the bold, daring statement of reinvention.

In my opinion, the chop is the ultimate hair therapy—transforming how you look on the outside to help shift how you feel on the inside. The risk is what makes it *fun*.

These Life Chops will leave you feeling lighter and more confident:

**Toxic Relationships:** It's often the most challenging cut to make, but one of the most essential. Just as your hairstyle can be weighed down by excess volume or split ends, your emotional life can grow too heavy with the wrong relationships. These people may have once contributed to your life in meaningful ways. But if they no longer lift or challenge you constructively, it's time to create distance and boundaries. If they cause you emotional, spiritual, mental, or physical harm, it's time to say goodbye. Your energy and your peace are sacred. Protect them.

**Old Beliefs and Self-Limiting Mindsets:** Just as we outgrow certain styles, so must we outgrow old beliefs. That voice telling you "You can't," or "You're not enough," needs to be shut down once and for all. These old narratives no longer align with the person you are evolving into. It's time to chop these beliefs like they're the last remnants of a terrible dye job.

**Dead End Jobs and Stagnant Careers:** You can tell if you're in the wrong job long before you probably will admit it to yourself. There are signs: lack of pay raise or promotions, no upward mobility opportunities on the horizon, the dread of going to work every day. Time to make a chop. You can quit, make that leap to a new department, or put in the work to follow your real dream—but it's most likely going to require a big change.

## THE THIRD OPTION: CONTOUR

Maybe you're at a place in your life where you really just want to enhance what's there instead of making all these cuts. If that's the case, what if I told you there was a third option?

My approach to cutting is often to CONTOUR hair to bring out the best features and reshape the story you want to tell.

If you've ever watched a makeup tutorial, you know that contouring isn't about changing who you are; it's about enhancing what's already there. In the same way that you highlight cheekbones or use dark tones to sculpt the jawline, you can contour your life to reveal your most dynamic version of yourself. Beyond getting rid of the bad, you can keep working on the good. Your strengths, passions, and ambitions can be shaped, highlighted, and brought into being.

**Mindset:** Confidence is the foundation upon which other growth is built. But confidence isn't something you're born with, and it isn't just something you earn from success. It's something you shape over time. Contour your mindset. Get rid of your negativity. Remind yourself of your worth and your abilities. These things can dramatically elevate every action you're already doing.

**Finances:** You might be in a career that's already allowed for you to reach a level of financial comfort, but for most, financial fear and instability are a huge challenge. Contouring your finances means getting clear and organized about your budget and refining your goals. When you align your financial reality to your needs and future plans, you're more likely to consider your spending and be more purposeful with saving or investing. Elevate what's already there by speaking with a financial advisor, watch the stock market, learn where to put your money to get the highest return and cut out the excess spending.

When deciding the next moves in your life, I know it's easy to get caught in a loop, overthinking decisions because you fear that you'll regret them later, or feel unable to decide because there is no clear and correct answer. Without certainty, not making a choice seems like the best decision.

But make no mistake:

### *No choice is still a choice.*

It's a choice to stay stuck. It's the choice to accept less. It's the choice to be unworthy of your own best effort, and how fucking sad is that?

Changing your hair and life requires different kinds of courage. Starting over isn't always starting from nothing. It's cutting the damage and cultivating health. The decision between the trim, the chop, and the contour isn't just about the physical acts, either. It's about how much of your emotional baggage you're ready to release.

Trim the clothes in your closet that you wore when you were at your lowest to make space for clothes that make you feel confident.

Chop the deadbeat guy who never calls, texts, or makes an effort, and get back out there so you can be open to someone who will.

Contour your schedule to prioritize following your passion, getting more sleep, or doing what makes you happy.

You decide when to trim, when to chop, and when to contour the things that affect your life, your look, and your ability to thrive.

# 16.

# That Voice Inside That Knows

*Listening to It—Even When You*
*Don't Like What It's Saying*

Everyone wants to be seen and loved. To have someone who is "their person." We are hardwired to seek connection with others; we crave attachment and a sense of belonging. To love and be loved. That's what life is all about, right?

When I think about the many relationships I've been in throughout my life, some have been good, some horrific, some were different than expected and altogether surprising. I've fallen in love with both women and men and had life-altering relationships with both. A few years ago, I even got married.

I was so sure I had found my person, that within a few months of being together, we got engaged. I was all in. We jetted off to Las Vegas with our families, were serenaded by Shania Twain, then wore matching fur coats as my dear friend Kim Kardashian officiated our wedding. The world watched it unfold on *The Kardashians*.

I believed in that love with my whole heart. I entered that marriage thinking it would last forever; that was my intent at the time. Unfortunately, that's not what happened. Almost as quickly as it began, it ended. We were divorced before the end of the year and went our separate ways. Yet I still believe in marriage and hope to be married again someday. I learned a lot about myself from every relationship I've been in, and I've lent an empathetic ear to hundreds, if not thousands, of people who have sat in my styling chair.

What I have learned from my clients, friends, and even my own experiences, is that we all fall for the fantasies of romance. We're led to believe that true love will complete you, that everyone has a soulmate. You're made to think that once you find "the one," everything will fall into place. You'll feel safe, seen, desired, completed. Your struggles will disappear because love will do the heavy lifting.

Yet, along with the blissful heavy lifting, you're also told to believe that *real* love is supposed to hurt. That's how you know it's *important*. But why does pain equate to importance?

A lot of that goes back to our roots. Perhaps the environment you were raised in or the relationships modeled for you were painful or abusive ones. When you're still carrying wounds from your roots and your past—childhood, relationships, traumas, insecurities—ten times out of ten you'll attract someone who *mirrors* them, not heals them. You tend to be attracted to what you know best, the familiar. But familiarity isn't always healthy.

I've been in relationships where I've felt loved and supported. I've also been in relationships where I've felt manipulated, confused, silenced, coerced into things I didn't want, or shaped into someone I wasn't meant to be. I've heard the voice of my intuition saying, *This isn't right. Get out.* I know what that voice sounds like; I've yielded to it before. I've also completely ignored it. I started over again at twenty-seven, and dating men was a steep learning curve for me.

I've been lonely, so emotionally starved, or bored, that I was susceptible to overlooking red flags as a trade-off for the intoxication of chemistry and intensity. I know I'm not alone in that. Like I said, I've been of counsel as a hairdresser/therapist for twenty-five years.

I have a pair of clients, who are now husband and wife, that I've been styling since they began dating. I had him as a client first, so I was aware of his previous relationships and dating history before meeting his wife. It's pretty common for my female clients to talk openly about their relationships, but most men who sit in my chair don't open up in the same way.

When he was in his early thirties, he was in a relationship that was so unhealthy, it pained me to hear him talk about it. It's easy to get seduced by the novelty of someone, especially when they're showing you the absolute best version of themselves, and that's what had happened to him. He fell for the most polished version of this woman, and eventually fell for the potential of her and their future.

But a few months in, things took a turn.

I'd hear about their relationship every six to eight weeks when he came in. At first, it was little things: she'd be critical of how quickly he ate; she wanted him to work out more. We discussed them as they were valid suggestions. Maybe she wanted their dinners together to last longer, and his eating speed made her feel pressured to match his pace, or she felt like she was eating alone while he waited. Maybe wanting him to work out more was for his overall health or to manage stress, and less about his body type.

But every time he came in, what he talked about seemed to be a growing list of complaints or criticisms. She didn't want him to go out with his friends without her anymore, and didn't like it when he laughed too loudly. He told me that she would cover her ears and say, "Could you not?"

I studied him silently, taking this in.

"It's fine. It's not a big deal. My mom always hated my dad's laugh. She would get so annoyed."

"That sounds awful," I told him. "Why would you want to be with someone who doesn't want you to laugh? Hearing the people I love laugh is one of my favorite sounds."

I'm not trying to villainize this woman, but I've known this man a long time, and he is ONE. OF. THE. GOOD. ONES. ALL CAPS.

Those warning signs were more obvious, but the truth is that unhealthy relationships don't always look dramatic from the outside. Sometimes, they're incredibly subtle. You lose pieces of yourself one compromise at a time. You begin adjusting your personality to avoid conflict. You second-guess your intuition. You tell yourself that things are okay when they aren't. I've done that numerous times.

But love is not supposed to make you shrink. True love allows you to expand. It invites your full self to the table—your joy, your mess, your past, your growth. If you feel like you're constantly trying to protect, prove, please, or appease, *that's not love.*

The next time he came in with yet another story like this, I finally said to him, "It doesn't sound like you're as compatible as you thought. What does that voice inside you have to say about all this?"

"But the good parts equal it all out," he rationalized.

"I'm sure you can make that math work for you, but that's not what I'm asking. What does your intuition tell you?"

There have been many times, even after I had spent so many years working on myself and untangling the issues from my past that haunted or inhibited me, that I still wasn't immune to some classic relationship bargaining. Not everyone is as self-aware or healed as they think.

He admitted to me that his intuition said he needed to end the relationship; his voice inside was speaking to him, but he didn't want to listen. He had already invested so much time in it. He had involved his friends and family in it, all of whom were skeptical about the two of them together, and he was embarrassed. He didn't want to face their judgment or I told you so's. The relationship wasn't just the two of them anymore; his ego and pride had become involved.

No relationship is perfect, and the reality of a relationship isn't found in how it looks on the outside. It's in the quiet, private moments where your gut tells you something's off, but you push that feeling aside because you *want* to believe. Or because you don't want to fail. The longer you deny the truth, the more painful the unraveling becomes.

Even when the intuitive voice inside you whispers, *Love should not feel like this*, it's natural to cling to the life rafts of avoidance, denial, and delusion. Your instinct might be to hold on tighter to the illusion. But truth has a funny way of rising slowly . . . and then, all at once.

I didn't see him for about six months. I wondered if I had overstepped with my opinions, and he had decided to find a new hairstylist. Then one day, I had a new client, a woman who had been given a hair appointment with me for her thirtieth birthday. She was lovely, with a kind of luminous quality and an ease that made me instantly like her.

She and I talked as I brightened her base and painted her highlights. She told me it was her boyfriend who had sent her to me and gifted this appointment.

"He's clearly a man with great taste," I joked.

"He's a man with great everything," she said beaming. "I'm really lucky. He sees me in a way no one has before, and I see him, too. He makes me feel understood and valued. What a concept, right?"

"That's all anyone could ask for."

"We share similar values, goals, and a common vision for life," she said sweetly. "Like everything just clicked, felt right, and made sense so quickly."

"He sounds wonderful. I'm happy for you." And I was. I

didn't know this person, but the bounce and bliss she had when she spoke of her boyfriend made me wistful for the same.

"Maybe you'll understand this better than me, but he said to tell you that I love the sound of his laugh . . . ? And I do, it's true. He has this big booming laugh, almost a snort, where his whole body shakes. It's the best."

I smiled.

"Where has he been? I thought he had broken up with me as his hairstylist."

"That's on me," she said sheepishly. "He told me he always wanted to have long hair and I told him he should let it grow."

She loved the thing about him that his last girlfriend had shamed him for, and was a voice of encouragement, not criticism. That's what healthy love looks like. When you find that, suddenly, the negativity of the past disappears, and all you can see is the future.

## THE ILLUSION OF LOVE AND THE REALITY OF BREAKUPS

It's easy to fall for the illusion of love. You get caught up when a relationship has that special spark, or the energy feels unstoppable. Who hasn't rushed into something too fast, only to have it crash and burn? Who hasn't been fixated on a particular person that you're sure is meant to be the one to fix you, complete you, or be the answer to all of your problems? The only one who can do those things for you, is you.

Everyone wants connection, partnership, excitement, and comfort in their life. With real love, those elements deepen over time; with the illusion of love, it's the opposite.

Maybe you confuse *chemistry* with the intoxication of *intensity*. You ignore the signs. You brush off the inconsideration. You internalize the hurt. You confuse attachment with emotional hunger.

You look to your love interest to provide things you should be able to provide yourself. You stay for what it was, not what it is.

It can be so hard to walk away or wave the white flag once you've committed to the idea that someone is your person, but ignoring what you know in your soul always costs you. Because unless you marry your childhood sweetheart, you're bound to get it wrong a few times before you get it right. Sometimes the person you pick is dysfunction dressed up as lust, or a trauma bond disguised as a twin flame. We are nothing if not creative in the people we attract, the excuses we make for them, and the way we hurt each other.

At this point in my life, I've gone through it myself and run the gamut with friends and relatives. I've stood on the outside of closed doors in disbelief, where words were said that couldn't be taken back. I watched people I love be wounded and worn down by their partners. I've been on the receiving end of treatment in countless relationships that I'm embarrassed to have allowed in my younger years, and witnessed even worse. It's easy to make excuses, point fingers, or assign blame when a relationship is falling apart—we all do it—but it's better to take a long, hard look at yourself.

Look inward with curiosity and compassion, not judgment. Consider yourself and your experiences holistically. It's all interconnected. What parts are still broken or damaged, attracting you to certain dynamics? Why do you tolerate being taken for granted or devalued? Why do you stay longer than you should? Why are you so afraid or ashamed to walk away?

The truth is, breaking generational cycles is such grueling work that most people will never do it. Think of all the beliefs you have to unlearn to finally feel worthy of the love you deserve. Leaving painfully familiar dynamics sounds like a no-brainer, but walking away is always more difficult than it looks.

You have to walk away, not just from a relationship or a person, but from a version of yourself. You have to choose healing over history, and healing means telling the truth—not just about others but yourself.

But let me say this clearly: leaving the wrong relationship for you isn't failure.

*It takes time to unlearn the idea
that endings are negative.*

Sometimes, they're the exact beginning you need. To return to yourself, to rediscover your boundaries and values, to reclaim your joy, your peace, and most importantly, your voice.

Your relationship with yourself sets the tone for everything else. If you're not grounded in self-worth, you'll overextend. You'll tolerate too much. You'll romanticize pain and drama. You'll stay because you're afraid to be alone. You'll confuse chaos for passion. And you'll call it love, because no one taught you better. But real, intentional self-reflection is what teaches you that peace is not boring, vulnerability is not weakness, and communication is not a constant form of confrontation.

I've had to hit the reset button and fall back in love with myself before. I've had to learn how to enjoy my own company again. How to take myself out to dinner. How to sit in silence. How to validate myself. That version of me is the person I spent my whole life searching for, but had to develop, grow, and heal to be found.

If you're in a relationship that doesn't feel good, trust that feeling. Listen to that voice inside you. You deserve better than constantly doubting yourself, walking on eggshells, or hiding pieces of who you are to please or keep someone.

Every day you concede your authentic and whole self for someone else and pretend to call it love is wasted time you don't get back.

Love is not a sacrifice of self. Love is expansion. Love is *I see you, and I still want to stay*, not *I'll stay if you become who I need you to be*. There's a big difference.

I used to think the right amount of love from someone else would enable me to love myself. Now I know if I don't love myself, I'll never attract a quality person capable of true, selfless love. I've become clear about what I need. I require trust, respect, consistency, emotional connectivity, self-awareness, someone who sees *me*, really sees me, not just the image, or what we'd look like together. I need someone whose love isn't conditional to me having to abandon myself, my morals, and my boundaries. I need someone who prioritizes me and us, who brings serenity, safety, and clear communication. I need to be complemented, not completed.

The best relationship I've ever had is the one I have with myself now. It came as much through embarrassments, failures, heartbreak, and loss as it came from resilience, determination, hard personal therapeutic work, and love. But it's real, it's me, and it's all mine.

I hope, wherever you are, whatever you've been or are going through, you know this is possible for you, too.

You're not broken. You're not behind. You're not too much or too late. You're right on time.

And you've always been worthy of a partner who elevates you, who isn't threatened by either your sense of self or your self-love.

# 17.

# The Head, the Hair, and the Heart

*Identifying the Emotional State*
*Behind Your Transformation*

One afternoon, a completely new client sat down in my chair, her eyes a little red, her shoulders tense. I had never met her before; this was her first appointment with me, but I could tell she was going through something major.

"Rough day?" I asked as I draped the cape over her.

"It's been a rough few years." She shrugged, her voice was thick with exhaustion and frustration. "I'm so fucking tired of holding it together. Not sure what you can do with this—" she lifted a section of her hair, glancing at me in the mirror "—but I need you just to do . . . something."

I nodded, understanding exactly what she meant. When life feels too heavy and stagnant, the one thing you can *immediately* change is your hair.

There's a visible string, I've always believed, that ties together the head, the heart, and the hair. When something shifts emotionally, it often finds its way to the hair. You'll see it in how people start cutting their hair impulsively after a breakup or in how someone suddenly goes from natural to platinum blonde after a significant life event. It's like changing your hair is a way to address the things you're not sure how to say out loud and can't seem to move through your body fast enough.

"I'm guessing you're not looking for just a trim?" I asked gently, though I already knew the answer.

She shook her head with a dry laugh. "No. It's going to take something more seismic."

A haircut wasn't going to solve everything, but it would be a start.

Her hair was long, dark, and lifeless, hanging down her back heavy with the burden of whatever she was carrying. There was no volume, no movement. I knew it needed to go.

I started with the cut. I trimmed off a good six inches, slicing through her hair with speed and precision. I tried to keep the conversation light as I worked, but it was entirely one-sided. She didn't utter a word. She just stared at herself in icy silence.

But I noticed something interesting: many of my clients will cringe or clench their hands when I start cutting, nervously anticipating the final result. With each section I cut, I could see her grip on the chair's armrests loosen. I knew she wasn't just letting go of the dead ends.

Her hair was softer, lighter, and more alive when I finished the cut. I added some loose, tousled waves with a curling iron to give it a bit of texture and movement.

"It feels like something's been lifted off," she said softly when I finished, brushing her fingers through the freshly cut layers. "I didn't realize how heavy it was."

"You don't realize how much you're holding until you finally take it off."

She stood up from the chair and asked if she could hug me. I opened my arms, and she walked into them. I hugged her tightly and felt the front of my T-shirt damp from her tears.

"You're going to be alright," I told her.

"I know," she said, "I just didn't believe it until now."

I still have no idea why she was in that place that day, but I don't need to know the details to see that she was walking out with more than a haircut when she left. She had severed something crushing.

That's how powerful the link between your head, your heart, and your hair can be.

I now want to spend some time cracking the code behind a few of the most common "reactionary haircuts" I've seen from my clients—and if any of these situations below apply to you, perhaps it's time to evaluate what kind of big, reactionary change is warranted in your own life—haircut or otherwise.

## THE BREAKUP HAIRCUT

There's an unspoken ritual that coincides with a breakup. It's when you're sitting in the wreckage of your love life, drowning yourself in booze, ice cream, hope-scrolling social media, looking for anything to distract you from the pain while *(500) Days of Summer, Eternal Sunshine of the Spotless Mind* and *He's Just Not That Into You* play on a continuous loop on your TV.

Some people disappear into the gym, some disappear into their beds, and others book the first available appointment at the salon. That's where I come in.

I've lost count of the number of clients who have sat in my chair with puffy red eyes, clutching their phones like a text will come through at any second to undo their pain. Without fail, they say the same words:

*I need something new.*

The change they need is never just about hair. It's a desperate craving for instant reinvention. I've had women sit in my chair and say, "Take it all off," as if cutting their long hair could erase the years they wasted loving someone who didn't love them back the way they deserved to be. Cut away the cheating. Cut away the ghosting. Cut away every scrap and memory of the person who hurt them.

A breakup is one of the most monumental upheavals you can have, regardless of what end of the breakup you are on (I say that having been on both). It disrupts every facet of your life in more ways than imaginable. Your heart is in complete shambles, and your routine is upended. Everywhere you once had stability—your apartment, your weekends, your friend group, your daily rhythms—you now have chaos. And you feel sick, literally ill all the time.

This turmoil is so insidious and destabilizing when everything is going to hell and falling apart, that something as simple as a haircut helps you emotionally regulate. You're taking charge.

In my experience, breakup haircuts are always some of the most dramatic. Cutting your hair post-breakup is a physical manifestation of emotional severance. It's a way to visually and emotionally separate from the person who broke your heart, to show yourself and the world that you will survive and thrive.

One of my most memorable breakup cuts came to me through a client. I got a 911 call from a reputable singer whose hair I've cut for the last seven years. "This is truly an emergency," she said. "You have to see my sister. She's leaving her husband and needs some hair courage immediately."

I went to my client's house and found her sister looking completely numb. No light in her eyes, no color in her face. I sat down next to her and said, "I have four hours and a bag full of color. We can do whatever you want to do, but by the look of things, we have to start right now."

It was as if she snapped out of a catatonic state. She looked at me and said, "I don't even know what I like by myself. I've been looking at everything through his eyes my entire adult life."

I handed her a mirror and said, "Then let's find you."

My friend put on a big pot of macaroni and cheese and pulled out every comfort food in the pantry while I set up my kit on the kitchen table. Her sister slumped into a chair, and the words spilled out of her.

She had been in a relationship for twelve years and married for ten of them. They were friends before things turned romantic, so the majority of her adult life was spent with him. Her identity had been so wrapped up in him: her work, her style, her TV shows. Even when she once wanted to cut her hair short, she kept it long because her husband liked it that way. He said he liked how it made her look like a famous actress. He made her feel beautiful. She had married her best friend. They always said from the beginning that they were each other's "end game".

Then, last night when she was using her husband's iPad, she saw intimate texts between him and a coworker from the Chicago branch of his job, with whom he was on a work retreat. He didn't know she knew yet.

She was devastated, looking for any sense of bravery and clarity to figure out what she was going to do next. She needed a visceral change in her nervous system. I know I had to do something with her hair that would give her a shot of strength every time she caught her reflection. Something that reminded her that her identity wasn't solely tied to anyone.

I painted babylights, bright blonde highlights, around her hairline, lifted the rest of her blonde with honey-gold highlights, and cut her hair into a chic jaw-length bob that was sharp and striking. It was a complete shift—something entirely hers.

She cried when she saw herself in the mirror and ran her hands through her hair, letting out the pent-up tension she had been holding. The cut didn't solve all of her relationship problems, obviously. But at that moment, in the comedown from a devastating, life-rupturing discovery, this simple change made her see herself differently, through her own lens, for the first time in years. "That's who I want to be from now on," she told me.

The breakup haircut is a rite of passage, a powerful symbol of transformation. If it weren't meaningful, we wouldn't see it depicted on screen as often as we do. Consider Carrie Bradshaw, Felicity, and Peggy Olson, among the many heartbroken or scorned protagonists emerging from breakups with new statement hair, as an act of defiance or survival. This cinematic reinvention resonates with us so profoundly because we've all been there in one way or another.

If you're in the middle of a breakup right now—or you suspect you might be heading into one—ask yourself what your own version of a breakup haircut could be. In my experience, one of the best things you can do is to transform the visible, familiar things you associate with that relationship. It helps reboot your nervous system. Simple things like moving your furniture around so you're not reminded of your partner's reading chair, switching your gym so you don't see him anymore, or using a different mug for your morning coffee.

And, of course, shake up your look. When you're hurting, you don't want to see the same, pained expression looking back in the mirror. Sometimes, changing your reflection is more manageable than facing what's underneath.

Or maybe you just need to sit in the chair, talk, and feel like you're taking back a little control in your life. Changing your hair color, getting a tattoo, and altering your look is about harnessing your capacity for moving on even when it's painful, and using a therapeutic act of self-care to propel yourself forward.

The breakup haircut is a way to process pain and regain control when spiraling. Everything we do in times of crisis should be in service to protecting, restoring, or chasing our light. Fresh hair gives us hope.

My breakup haircut came when I finally faced my truth and came out to my girlfriend, children, and my parents. Looking in the mirror, I didn't recognize myself anymore. I hadn't changed physically, but I was seeing an old version of myself. I was ready to embrace the new one, so I took the scissors out and began cutting.

In some ways, I was grieving the man who tried so hard to be the perfect boyfriend and the father who wanted to be "normal" for his kids—a role I'd played so convincingly that I even believed it for a time. But I was also changing my hair as a symbolic statement of the man I would be as I began to live my authentic self.

The truth is, reinvention doesn't erase pain. A haircut won't make you forget about someone you loved, but it can remind you of who you are without them. Hair grows back, and hearts mend.

The real magic of the breakup haircut isn't in the scissors or the dye. It's the step toward healing and reclaiming your story. It's the moment when you see yourself and realize that you are still you—and you are going to be okay.

## THE REVENGE HAIRCUT

There are times when the scissors feel heavier in my hands. It's not because of their weight, but because of the power they hold. A haircut can be many things: a fresh start, a transformation, a statement. There's one kind of haircut that carries an entirely different energy.

You've likely heard of the "Revenge Dress" and the "Revenge Body," especially with those who have *been through it* publicly. Rounding out the trifecta is the "Revenge Haircut." This one isn't fueled by heartbreak but rather anger. It's a little more intense, more pointed, a little *gritty*. It's the "fuck you" of haircuts. It's directed at something or someone.

It's a haircut that says, *You can't hurt me anymore* or *I'd rather be slashing your tires.*

You know the feeling: someone crossed you, betrayed you, or fucked you over. A shitty friend, a horrible job environment, or a past lover did you dirty, and there's nothing to do but hold your head high while you swallow the hurt or humiliation.

This haircut isn't just about feeling better for yourself. The revenge haircut is about everyone else *seeing* you pull it together when they didn't expect you could. The ultimate payback isn't taking down the person who wronged you; it's about sending the message that you are untouchable. This message of strength and invincibility is as much for you as it is for anyone else.

Until the wounds heal or the betrayal and humiliation fade, find something that feels like a bold statement for you: one that sends the message that you've stopped caring what anyone else thinks, especially with a middle finger to the person who wronged you. Whether it's buying a leather jacket that's edgier than your usual wardrobe, booking a solo trip abroad for a week, getting the laser-eye surgery you've always wanted, but people advised you not to get because "glasses was more *you*"—this change is your victory lap.

Cashing in on that revenge transformation feels empowering and exciting, which are precisely the feelings you need coursing through your veins. Taking your power back by taking control of your image can turn you from feeling like a victim to a victor.

One particular revenge haircut stands out to me above the others. It was the way this woman in her late twenties, dressed in a power skirt suit, walked in with this searing determination that I could feel before she even spoke. Her long, honey-blonde waves cascaded past her shoulders, polished and perfect, almost like they belonged in a shampoo commercial.

She sat in my chair, met my eyes in the mirror, and said, "Cut it all off."

I spun her chair to face me instead of the mirror. "Talk to me first about what's going on and what you're hoping to feel when we're done."

Her story poured out like a confession. Her boss, a controlling man at a top law firm, had a very strict dress code for his employees. He dictated how she should dress and wear her hair—always long, always feminine, always meticulous. It was how he wanted his company represented. She was his executive assistant and he kept her on a short leash under the guise of special mentorship.

The relationship and power dynamic had become emotionally abusive. She felt depressed, insecure, and drained all the time and barely recognized herself.

She had secretly contacted a recruiter and had gone through a long interview process with a company she was excited about. She was finally offered the job and didn't have to start for another three weeks. After booking a vacation to Greece with her best friend and a haircut, she was ready to take her life back.

I smiled. This haircut would be about reclaiming who she was moving forward. It would be the armor she would wear into her controlling boss's office mere hours from now when she resigned.

I could see her power flooding into her body with every snip. I took four inches off her honey-blonde waves so they reached her shoulders—far shorter than her boss would've wanted—and contoured textured face-framing layers that she could wash and wear. She would never spend another second under a blow-dryer or curling iron if she didn't choose to.

She tilted her head from side to side, shaking out her new hair. "It's perfect," she whispered. "I've got a job to quit."

I watched her walk out of the salon that day, shoulders back, head high, confidently stepping back into herself and her next chapter. When she came back months later for a trim, I asked about her new job. She replied that it was fantastic (as was her vacation). I asked her how quitting her job was.

She replied, "It was the single most satisfying moment of my life. Your haircut made me a force of nature. He did not see that coming."

## THE IMPULSE BANGS

Getting bangs won't fix your life. You would not believe how many times I've had to repeat this sentence to clients.

We've all been there, scissors in hand, heart full of chaos, wondering if bangs would solve everything—get us out of the rut, heal the existential crisis, make us feel younger or cooler. When someone says, "I want bangs," I've found they usually mean "I want to feel different *right now*."

There are few moments as universally relatable as this impulse. Cutting bangs is the cultural shorthand for an emotional reboot. A visual metaphor that says, *I'm making questionable decisions, but I'm doing it on purpose. What you're seeing here is me turning a corner.*

When your life feels stuck or in shambles, cutting your bangs is an act of empowerment . . . but also, let's be honest, it's usually a sign of personal crisis or existential dread. Your job sucks, or worse, you've been fired, your ex is posting thirst traps on Instagram, your dog died, your favorite dish broke, and your mental health is teetering on the edge. But you could always get bangs, right?! It's comforting to know that you can pull the trigger on a radical change at a moment's notice. It's the promise of instant transformation.

The bangs call to you like a compulsive thought. You stand in front of the mirror, scissors in hand, your agency coursing through you like electricity. A small act of defiance against a world in which we feel powerless.

*Snip. Snip. Snip . . .*

And just like that, you've got bangs. Or something that resembles bangs.

If you're in a rut, then maybe your version of this—whatever will bring that seismic change to your life to get you out—can be achieved by something else: get a piercing. Try being vegetarian for a week. Adopt a pet and become a dog dad. Plan a cross-country trip this summer. Find something that brings a "before and after" to your life, and which can trigger that shift between who you were and who you want to be.

Whatever it is, proceed with caution. There's always risk when you impulsively make a significant change—your moment of "breaking free" can devolve into a world of regret if you're not intentional and clear with what you want. Whatever it is you decide to transform, I advise taking a friend with you. When it comes to hair, at least, I've lost count of the number of clients who have come to me with a completely botched hairstyle after their epiphany, so do your research on what kind of lifestyle and maintenance your impulse bangs are going to require.

Sometimes, the damage can be fixed with another cut, and sometimes it's a painful waiting game. The only thing that will help is growth, and growth takes time.

# 18.

# Cutting Iconic Bangs

*A Style Guide*

Now, let's say your version of "impulse bangs" really are getting literal bangs.

I can't stop you from cutting your own hair in a moment of inspiration or desperation. But what I can do is help you cut them correctly. Bangs can be iconic or tragic, and in either case, they change your whole look. Picking a muse for your bangs will increase your chances of cutting bangs that give you confidence, not have you reaching for the nearest hat.

## THE STYLES

### French Fringe

*French Fringe* (also known as a Birkin Bang or Parisian Fringe—seen on Daisy Edgar-Jones/Zendaya) is a soft, effortless, and slightly grown-out bang style. It's characterized by:

- **Wispy texture:** Not too thick or blunt, allowing it to blend seamlessly into the rest of the hair.
- **Face-framing effect:** Slightly longer on the sides to create a flattering, natural shape.
- **Low-maintenance feel:** Unlike blunt bangs, this fringe is meant to look a bit tousled and effortless.

### *How to Cut French Fringe at Home*

You'll Need:

☐ Sharp hair-cutting scissors
☐ A fine-tooth comb
☐ Sectioning clips
☐ A spray bottle with water

### Step 1: Section the Hair

- Start with dry hair (so you can see the natural fall).
- Use a fine-tooth comb to create a triangle section, with the widest part of the triangle at your temples and the point at the top of your head.
- Clip back the rest of your hair to avoid cutting too much.

### Step 2: Determine the Length

- For a Daisy Edgar-Jones look, the center should hit just below your eyebrows, with the sides slightly longer.
- If unsure, start longer—you can always trim more later.

### Step 3: Cut Vertically for Softness

- Hold the sectioned hair between your fingers and twist it slightly (this helps create a soft, feathered effect).
- Using your scissors, point-cut vertically instead of straight across to create a wispy finish.

### Step 4: Blend the Sides

- Release a small amount of hair from the sides and point-cut diagonally so it blends into the rest of your hair.

- The outer edges should graze your cheekbones for that effortless French look.

## Step 5: Style It

- Blow-dry using a round brush or your fingers, lifting slightly at the roots.
- A light spritz of dry shampoo or texture spray will enhance the undone, Parisian feel.

## Bottleneck Bangs

*Bottleneck Bangs* (seen on Halle Berry/Lily Collins) are a modern, versatile fringe that combines the softness of curtain bangs with the shape of a bottleneck—narrow at the top and widening toward the cheekbones. This creates a face-framing effect that works on many face shapes.

Key Features of Bottleneck Bangs:

- **Narrow at the center:** The shortest part sits between the eyebrows or just below.
- **Gradual lengthening:** The bangs get longer as they move toward the cheekbones, blending into the rest of the hair.
- **Soft, feathery texture:** Unlike blunt bangs, these are slightly choppy and effortless.

### *How to Cut Bottleneck Bangs at Home*

You'll Need:

- ☐ Sharp hair-cutting scissors
- ☐ A fine-tooth comb
- ☐ Sectioning clips
- ☐ A spray bottle with water

### Step 1: Section the Hair

- Start with dry hair so you can see its natural fall.
- Create a triangular section at the front, starting from your temples and meeting at a point at the top of your head.

### Step 2: Cut the Center First

- Take the middle section (about an inch wide) and determine your shortest length—usually between the eyebrows and the bridge of the nose.
- Hold the hair between your fingers and point-cut vertically (never straight across) for a soft look.

### Step 3: Blend the Sides

- Release the next sections on either side of the center. These should be cut slightly longer, reaching the tops of the cheekbones.
- Use diagonal point-cutting to create a gradual length increase.

### Step 4: Connect to the Rest of the Hair

- The outermost sections should blend into your face-framing layers. Cut these at a downward angle to create that "bottleneck" widening effect.

### Step 5: Style It

- Blow-dry using a round brush, lifting the roots slightly for volume.
- Use a small curling iron or straightener to bend the ends inward for a soft, effortless shape.

- A light spritz of texture spray or dry shampoo will add movement.

## Full Bangs

*Full Bangs* (seen on Zooey Deschanel and Lisa from BLACK-PINK) are full, blunt, and ultrapolished. They create a statement look with thick, structured fringe that fully covers the forehead. These bangs are perfect for those who want a bold, eye-catching style with a classic and youthful feel.

These are the characteristics of full bangs:

- **Thick & heavy:** Unlike wispy bangs, these are cut thick to create density.
- **Blunt & straight:** The ends are cut in a straight line for a sharp, polished look.
- **Covers the forehead completely:** No gaps or parting in the middle.

### How to Cut Full Bangs at Home

You'll Need:

- ☐ Sharp hair-cutting scissors
- ☐ A fine-tooth comb
- ☐ Sectioning clips
- ☐ A flat iron (for styling)

### Step 1: Section the Hair

- Start with dry hair so you can see its natural fall.
- Create a deep triangular section at the front of your head, from temple to temple. The deeper the triangle, the thicker the bangs.
- Clip back the rest of your hair.

### Step 2: Determine the Length

- The ideal length is just below the eyebrows or slightly grazing them.
- If you're unsure, start longer—you can always trim more.

### Step 3: Cut the Bangs

- Hold the section straight down in front of your face.
- Using scissors parallel to your forehead, cut straight across in small snips to avoid a harsh line.
- For Zooey Deschanel's bangs, keep them thick and slightly rounded at the edges.
- For Lisa's bangs, keep them razor-sharp and ultra-blunt.

### Step 4: Refine the Shape

- If you want a soft, rounded effect, trim the edges slightly shorter toward the middle.
- For a super blunt look, keep the edges crisp and straight.

### Step 5: Style It

- Blow-dry using a flat brush, brushing the bangs side to side for a smooth finish.
- Use a flat iron to lightly curve the ends inward for a polished look.
- Apply a tiny bit of dry shampoo to keep them fresh and oil-free.

**Curtain Bangs**

*Curtain Bangs* (seen on Taylor Swift/Camila Cabello) are effortlessly chic, face-framing bangs that part in the middle and softly blend into the rest of the hair. These bangs give a soft, romantic, and slightly retro feel, making them one of the most universally flattering fringe styles.

Key Features of Curtain Bangs:

- **Middle-parted:** They naturally split in the center and sweep to the sides instead of covering the whole forehead.
- **Soft & feathery:** Unlike blunt bangs, these have a wispy, lived-in look.
- **Longer on the sides:** The shortest point is around the eyebrows, gradually blending into face-framing layers.

### How to Cut Curtain Bangs at Home

You'll Need:

- ☐ Sharp hair-cutting scissors
- ☐ A fine-tooth comb
- ☐ Sectioning clips
- ☐ A round brush & blow-dryer

### Step 1: Section the Hair

- Start with dry hair (curtain bangs shrink when cut wet).
- Create a triangle section at the front, starting from your temples and meeting at a point near the crown.
- Clip the rest of your hair back.

### Step 2: Cut the Shortest Part First

- Take the middle section (the part that will sit between your brows).

- Hold the hair at a slight downward angle and point-cut to just below the eyebrows.
- Always cut longer than you think—you can refine later!

### Step 3: Blend the Sides

- Release small sections on each side.
- Hold them at a diagonal angle and point-cut so they gradually lengthen toward the cheekbones or jawline.
- These should blend smoothly into your layers for a seamless look.

### Step 4: Style It

- Blow-dry using a round brush, rolling the bangs away from your face.
- Use a straightener or curling iron to enhance the swooping effect.
- Finish with texturizing spray or dry shampoo for volume and hold.

**Micro Bangs**

*Micro Bangs* (also called baby bangs or mini bangs—seen on Zoë Kravitz/Kristen Stewart) are a bold and edgy style where the fringe is cut significantly shorter than traditional bangs. They create a striking, high-fashion look that emphasizes the eyebrows and facial features.

Key Features of Micro/Mini Bangs:

- **Ultra-short length:** Typically falls between the mid-forehead and just above the eyebrows.
- **Blunt or textured:** Can be cut sharply for a statement look or slightly choppy for a softer effect.

- **High-impact style:** Works best on oval, heart, and angular face shapes.

### How to Cut Micro Bangs at Home

You'll Need:

- ☐ Sharp hair-cutting scissors
- ☐ A fine-tooth comb
- ☐ Sectioning clips
- ☐ A flat iron for styling

### Step 1: Section the Hair

- Start with dry hair to see the true length.
- Create a small triangle section at the front, from temple to temple.
- Clip back the rest of your hair to avoid cutting too much.

### Step 2: Determine the Length

- For Zoë Kravitz's style, aim for mid-forehead for a bold, high-fashion look.
- For Kristen Stewart's version, keep it slightly softer and choppy, just above the brows.

### Step 3: Cut the Bangs

- Hold the section down naturally (no pulling) and cut straight across if you want a blunt look.
- For a softer, more textured style, point-cut vertically in small snips to create a feathery effect.
- If you're unsure, start longer—you can always trim more!

## Step 4: Adjust the Edges

- Keep the edges slightly uneven for a lived-in feel or perfectly straight for a sharper aesthetic.
- If desired, lightly taper the outer edges so they blend into your face-framing layers.

## Step 5: Style It

- Blow-dry with a small round brush or use a flat iron for a sleek, polished look.
- Add a bit of texturizing spray for an edgy, effortless finish.
- For extra definition, lightly piece out sections with styling wax.

## Bardot Bangs

*Bardot Bangs* (seen on Jennifer Lopez/Sabrina Carpenter) are named after French icon Brigitte Bardot, and are effortlessly sexy, voluminous, and softly feathered. This style is all about a relaxed, undone look that frames the face beautifully while blending seamlessly into the rest of the hair.

Key Features of Bardot Bangs:

- **Long, wispy, & parted in the center:** Creates a soft, face-framing effect.
- **Gradual length:** Shortest point around the eyes, blending into longer layers at the cheekbones or jawline.
- **Flirty & voluminous:** Often styled with a bit of bounce for a glamorous, '60s-inspired vibe.

### *How to Cut Bardot Bangs at Home*

You'll Need:

- ☐ Sharp hair-cutting scissors
- ☐ A fine-tooth comb
- ☐ Sectioning clips
- ☐ A round brush & blow-dryer

### Step 1: Section the Hair

- Start with dry hair to see how it naturally falls.
- Create a triangle section starting from your temples and meeting at a point at the top of your head.
- Clip back the rest of your hair.

### Step 2: Cut the Shortest Section

- Take the center of the triangle (about an inch wide) and determine the shortest point—usually around the bridge of the nose or slightly above the eyes.
- Hold the hair at a slight downward angle and point-cut vertically for a soft, feathery effect.

### Step 3: Blend the Sides

- Release small sections on each side and cut them at a diagonal angle, gradually increasing the length as you reach the cheekbones.
- Keep the edges wispy and soft by using point-cutting instead of a blunt chop.

### Step 4: Style for Volume

- Blow-dry using a round brush, sweeping the bangs away from the face to create movement.

- Use a curling iron or large rollers to add a slight bend for that effortless Bardot bounce.
- Finish with texture spray or dry shampoo to enhance the undone, voluminous effect.

**Curve Bangs**

*Curve Bangs* (seen on Jenna Ortega/Dakota Johnson) are soft, full, and naturally frame the face by curving gently inward. This style creates a seamless transition between the bangs and the rest of the hair, offering a flattering and effortless look. They add dimension while maintaining movement, making them versatile for different hair textures and lengths.

Key Features of Curve Bangs:

- **Soft & full:** Not too blunt, with a natural curve that blends into face-framing layers.
- **Slightly longer on the sides:** This helps the bangs transition smoothly into the rest of the hair.
- **Works well with waves or straight styles:** A flattering option for both polished and tousled looks.

*How to Cut Curve Bangs at Home*

You'll Need:

- ☐ Sharp hair-cutting scissors
- ☐ A fine-tooth comb
- ☐ Sectioning clips
- ☐ A round brush & blow-dryer

Step 1: Section the Hair

- Start with dry hair to see how it naturally falls.

- Create a triangular section starting from your temples and meeting at a point near the crown.
- Clip back the rest of your hair.

### Step 2: Cut the Shortest Section First

- Take the center section of the bangs and determine the length—usually just below the eyebrows.
- Hold the hair at a slight downward angle and point-cut vertically for a soft, blended effect.

### Step 3: Create the Curve Shape

- Release the side sections and cut them slightly longer, angling downward toward the cheekbones.
- Use point-cutting to remove weight while keeping a feathery texture.

### Step 4: Style for the Perfect Curve

- Blow-dry using a round brush, rolling the bangs inward and slightly to the sides.
- Use a flat iron or curling iron to bend the ends for a soft, curved effect lightly.
- Finish with light hairspray or texturizing spray for movement and hold.

### Long Bangs

*Long Bangs* (seen on Emily Ratajkowski/Priyanka Chopra Jonas) are effortlessly chic, giving a sultry, face-framing effect without the commitment of shorter bangs. They blend seamlessly into the rest of the hair, offering versatility—whether worn down, tucked behind the ears, or styled into soft waves.

Key Features of Long Bangs:

- **Long & layered:** Usually fall between the cheekbones and jawline.
- **Soft & feathery:** Not too thick or blunt—meant to move naturally.
- **Easily blendable:** Can be styled as curtain bangs, swept to the side, or tucked away.

### How to Cut Long Bangs at Home

You'll Need:

- ☐ Sharp hair-cutting scissors
- ☐ A fine-tooth comb
- ☐ Sectioning clips
- ☐ A round brush & blow-dryer

### Step 1: Section the Hair

- Start with dry hair to see its natural fall.
- Create a deep triangular section from your temples to a point at the top of your head.
- Clip back the rest of your hair.

### Step 2: Determine the Length

- The shortest point should start around the cheekbones, with the longest pieces blending into the jawline.
- If unsure, start longer (around the jaw) and trim gradually.

### Step 3: Cut in a Soft, Angled Shape

- Hold the center section between your fingers and point-cut vertically to remove weight.
- Move outward, cutting the side sections at a diagonal angle, making the length longer as you move toward the rest of the hair.
- Keep the edges soft and wispy by avoiding blunt cuts.

### Step 4: Style for Movement

- Blow-dry using a round brush, rolling the bangs away from the face for a natural, face-framing curve.
- Use a curling iron or flat iron to add subtle waves for an effortless, tousled look.
- Apply light texturizing spray for an undone, effortless finish.

# 19.

# Dye It, Change It, Own It

*Finding Your Hair Personality (and Other Style Tips for Putting in the Work)*

A few years ago when I was doing an artist in residence appearance at a salon in London for one of my brand partners, a woman in her early thirties came in with that look I've seen a hundred times before—half defeated, half desperate, like she was hoping I had a magic wand hidden in my kit.

"Just tell me what to do," she said, tugging at her hair like it had personally failed her. "Tell me what products to buy. I don't have perfect bone structure and flawless skin like a celebrity. I just have what you see to work with. I don't even know where to start. I can't keep up. I'm literally . . . lost."

Her voice cracked a little on that last word.

And just like that, it stopped being about hair.

What she was really saying was: I don't feel beautiful. I don't feel worthy. I don't feel good in my skin. I don't feel seen. I don't feel confident. I don't feel like these feelings will ever change.

This kind of moment doesn't come with a dramatic makeover montage. It comes quietly, in the hum of the salon, when someone is vulnerable enough to finally say what they've been holding in. Feeling good enough is impossible when you're constantly being inundated with other people's beauty and success.

But here's what I've learned after years in this industry:

*The most toxic lie you've been sold*
*is the idea of effortless beauty.*

Because *nothing* about the "effortless" looks you see on Instagram, red carpets, or glossy magazine covers is actually effortless. Those looks are the result of five hours in a glam chair, a team of top stylists, makeup artists, assistants, lighting experts, wardrobe stylists, and photographers—and then, of course, a little Photoshop (or a lot of Photoshop) to top it all off.

No one's waking up in the morning with a fresh blowout, dewy skin, sculpted cheekbones, and a perfect pout, with their hair magically falling into place. It's all smoke, mirrors, filters, and a meticulously curated eye. But simply knowing that to be the truth won't stop your insecurities from flaring up.

Listen closely: even the women or people you compare yourself to . . . are comparing themselves to someone else.

They're looking in the mirror, seeing a reality that doesn't make the grade because we've become programmed to desire poreless, even skin, smoothed-out wrinkles, glossy hair, and perfect brows. It's a hamster wheel. And it's exhausting.

So, I told her what I always remind my clients of: "You're not *supposed* to look like them. Period. They don't even look like that without help."

It's the truth. I have been behind the scenes with some of the most beautiful women for the Met Gala and *Vogue* cover shoots, and I've been with them for an outing to the grocery store. They all start with a blank face and wet hair—just like you and I do.

Getting the look you want takes *work* to regular take care of your skin and hair and body. (That, and literal face work.) Celebrities use the best skin and hair care products because they have worked hard to afford them. They know all the glam tips and tricks because they've picked them up or been taught by the best. They put in the effort daily because maintaining their image and looks is often imperative for their employment or brands.

That day, I looked my client in the eye and said, "You need to stop worrying about trying to emulate those celebrities and just concentrate on finding the best version of yourself—one that feels powerful, not pressured."

I didn't do a big overhaul or give her an impossible routine. I gave her a cut that brought life back to her features, lightening the color just enough to soften and brighten her skin tone. We talked about what products she actually had time to use, what products worked with her actual hair texture, and what products she could afford—*not what some influencer with three assistants and a ring light was using.*

While working on her hair, I could see the defeat leaving her body. She could see herself again. Not as a project to fix or as a comparison to an unrealistic ideal, but as someone who simply liked what they saw in the mirror.

That's the gift of this job. Not creating an illusion, but helping someone rediscover their reality—and fall in love with it.

All of these celebrities or influencers have one thing in common: they've given themselves permission to try new things. They aren't tied to one look forever. Look at all the ways that they can change their hair and image as often as they change their clothes.

That freedom and confidence is aspirational—that is the thing you respond to.

I always tell my friends and clients that hair is the best place to start being brave. It's visible, it's changeable, and you can experiment easily. A new cut or color doesn't just change how you look; it resets your energy. It helps you let go of the version of yourself you've outgrown. That courage spills over into the rest of your life.

Suddenly, you're not just trying a new style. You're reclaiming space, taking up more room, and making more noise.

The same questions pop up daily in my DMs and comments on my social media accounts. People desperate to learn the secrets of those they admire, whose lives, by all appearances, seem better than their own.

*How can I have what they have?*

*How can I look like they look?*

*How can I feel what they feel?*

*Tell me what I need.*

*Tell me what will look good on me.*

The answer to these questions is the same: confidence and a great haircut.

If you've ever felt like you're not measuring up, let me tell you what I tell my clients:

*You're not falling short.*

*You're just looking in the wrong direction.*

*You don't need to look like someone else to be beautiful.*

All you need is to look like yourself—the confident, intentional, and real version of yourself that you are rebuilding now that you've torn down all your obstacles, old beliefs, and road-blocks.

And if I haven't said it clearly or often enough: *fuck perfection.* Perfection is a myth, but confidence is transformative. And the kind of confidence you're giving yourself by leading with your truth is the kind of beauty that doesn't need five hours and a full glam team.

Maybe you've had the same comfortable but tired haircut forever that you consider your "signature style," or you're using your hair as a shield or a Do Not Disturb sign to hide behind.

Isn't it time you took a lesson from the playbook of those you envy or admire?

*Where's the excitement?* How much longer do you intend to stay hidden? Your hair should be a playground, not a prison! Your story, like your hair, deserves to be dynamic and evolving. Yours is a story of courage, adaptability, and zest for life.

## FIND YOUR STYLE PERSONALITY

There are three main hair personality types: **The Muse**, **The Trendsetter**, and **The Icon**. Let's take a short quiz below to determine which one you are and how it can help you capitalize on the best aesthetic choices that feel truest to your energy and essence.

Question: How do you usually decide on your hairstyle?

**a.** I like to stick to what I know suits me.

**b.** I keep an eye on next season's runway collections and experiment with versions of it.

**c.** I like to do the exact opposite of what's expected and make it my own.

Question: What's your ideal hair transformation?

**a.** A subtle refresh that looks healthy and polished.

**b.** A fresh cut or color that's ahead of the trend.

**c.** A bold new shape or shade that no one saw coming.

Question: How often do you change your look?

**a.** Rarely, I love consistency.

**b.** Once or twice a year.

**c.** Constantly, I get bored easily.

Question: What kind of impression do you want your hair to leave?

**a.** That I'm put together, natural, and effortless.

**b.** That I'm fun, fashionable, and cool.

**c.** That I'm a walking piece of art.

Question: When you're scrolling for hair inspo, what grabs you?

**a.** Clean cuts, glossy blowouts, minimal effort.

**b.** Soft layers, impactful bangs, caramel tones.

**c.** Bleached blondes, high contrast color, blunt shapes.

Question: What's your biggest fear when it comes to your hair?

**a.** Doing too much and regretting it.

**b.** Falling behind the curve instead of setting it.

**c.** Looking like anyone else.

Question: When you enter a party, are you more:

**a.** The observer who finds a quiet corner and takes it all in.

**b.** The connector that brings people together.

**c.** The main character who makes the party an event.

Question: How do you feel about trends?

**a.** I ignore them—they feel too loud.

**b.** I filter them through my style.

**c.** I'm already wearing next year's trend.

Now tally up your answers:

*Mostly A's = You're the Muse*

Polished, timeless, and subtle. You love clean, classic hair that whispers confidence without trying too hard. You want your hair to support, not steal, the show. You're not into drastic changes. Your vibe is quiet luxury, clean lines, soft shapes, healthy ends, and colors that melt into each other. You prefer timeless over trendy.

**Hair Signature:** Glossy natural tones, classic cuts, un-done elegance. Think in terms of: barely-there balayage, polished blowouts, clean bobs, natural partings.

**Celebrity Examples:** Zoë Kravitz (quiet cool), Jennifer Garner (girl-next-door chic), Sofia Coppola (artsy mini-malism), Gwyneth Paltrow (minimalist elegance), Helen Mirren (classic with ageless grace), Jessica Alba (casual cool with a polished edge).

**Your Mantra:** "Don't notice me for my hair. Just know I look good."

*Mostly B's = You're the Trendsetter*

You're playful, confident, and forward-thinking. You love reinventing your look just enough to keep it fresh—not too safe, not too wild. You're up-to-date and always on point. You're the one people scroll TikTok to see for inspo, and you're always three steps ahead of your friend group when it comes to hair or fashion trends. You don't want to look like everyone else, but you also don't mind borrowing from the moment.

**Hair Signature:** Butterfly cuts, curtain bangs, caramel pops, trending tones. You're always experimenting, but within a zone of "still wearable."

**Celebrity Examples:** Hailey Bieber (quintessential It girl), Amanda Seyfried (modern classic), Kim Kardashian (chocolate brunette phase), Zendaya (chameleon cool), Tracee Ellis Ross (confident eclectic), Michelle Obama (edgy chic strong).

**Your Mantra:** "Let's try it—but make it me."

### Mostly C's = You're the Icon

Bold. Unapologetic. Reinvented. You go big or go home. Hair is a mood, a statement, a headline. You're not following trends—you're rewriting them. When you walk in, people know. Your hair is an exclamation point, an extension of your fearless energy.

**Hair Signature:** Platinum buzz cuts, vivid color blocks, razor-sharp lines, layered extensions, edgy styling.

**Celebrity Examples:** Chappell Roan (unapologetic camp), Billie Eilish (neon era), Rihanna (every era), Tilda Swinton (alien goddess energy), Cynthia Erivo (fearless in color, texture, and scale), Colman Domingo (dramatic, elegant), Florence Pugh (daring, edgy).

**Your Mantra:** "If everyone's going left, I'm going right AND I'm going neon."

*Hybrid Types (Because we're complex
humans with layers.)*

**Quiet Icon:** Someone with classic but cool elegance,
who often drops a LOOK that leaves jaws on the floor.
Think: Michelle Williams, Lupita Nyong'o, Cate Blanchett,
Ruth Negga.

**Luxe Trendsetter:** Tasteful layers of personality—luxury
details, subtle edge. Think: Alexa Chung, Solange Knowles,
Demi Moore.

**Power Muse:** Classic lines and natural hues, but you
*know* they know who they are. Think: Meghan Markle,
Rooney Mara, Zoe Saldaña.

## FINDING THE BEST HAIRCUTS FOR YOUR FACE

The right haircut is about balance. It should enhance your best
features while complementing your unique face shape. I can't
be with you at the salon, but I can give you my opinion on cuts
that will flatter that beautiful head of yours.

### Oval Face (Balanced, Slightly Longer Than Wide)

Almost any style works, but volume and structure are key.

**Best cuts:** Soft layers, long bobs, textured cuts.

**Best for men:** Classic quiff, pompadour, undercut.

### Round Face (Full Cheeks, Equal Width & Length)

Add angles and elongation with longer hairstyles and layers.

**Best cuts:** Sideswept bangs, face-framing layers.

**Best for men:** Faux hawk, textured quiff (avoid buzz cuts).

## Square Face (Strong Jawline, Equal Width & Length)

Soften harsh angles with layers and waves.

**Best cuts:** Curtain bangs, side parts, soft layers.

**Best for men:** Pompadour, slicked-back styles.

## Heart-Shaped Face (Wide Forehead, Tapered Jawline)

Balance the jawline with chin-length or wavy styles.

**Best cuts:** Wispy bangs, side parts, bobs.

**Best for men:** Mid-length styles with texture.

## Diamond Face (Narrow Forehead & Jaw, Wide Cheekbones)

Add width at the jawline with soft, layered styles.

**Best cuts:** Shoulder-length waves, textured styles.

**Best for men:** Side-swept or layered cuts (avoid too-short sides).

## Oblong/Rectangular Face (Longer Than Wide, Strong Jawline & Forehead)

Avoid too much height—go for balanced volume on the sides.

**Best cuts:** Curtain bangs, soft layers, shoulder-length waves.

**Best for men:** Textured side parts, medium-length styles (avoid slicked-back looks).

## CHOOSING A HAIR COLOR THAT FLATTERS

The right hair color enhances your skin tone and eye color without washing you out or aging you. Here's a reference guide to help you choose the best hair color for you.

### Skin Tone

Hair Color for Fair Skin with Cool
Undertones (Pink or Blueish Tint)

- **Best:** Platinum blonde (Gwen Stefani), Ash blonde (Taylor Swift), Cool brown (Anne Hathaway), Jet-black (Dita Von Teese)
- **Avoid:** Warm reds, brassy blondes that clash with cool undertones

Hair Color for Fair Skin with Warm
Undertones (Peachy or Golden Tint)

- **Best:** Golden blonde (Margot Robbie), Honey blonde (Blake Lively), Copper red (Jessica Chastain), Warm brown (Kate Middleton)
- **Avoid:** Ashy tones that can wash out warmth in the skin

Hair Color for Medium Skin with Cool
Undertones (Pink or Blueish Tint)

- **Best:** Rich chocolate brown (Lily Aldridge), Cool caramel (Olivia Munn), Dark ashy blonde (Jennifer Aniston's darker blonde)
- **Avoid:** Too-warm shades like orange-toned blondes

## Hair Color for Medium Skin with Warm Undertones (Peachy or Golden Tint)

- **Best:** Golden honey (Beyoncé), Warm chestnut brown (Jennifer Lopez), Auburn (Eva Mendes), Rich caramel (Priyanka Chopra Jonas)
- **Avoid:** Overly ashy tones that dull warmth in the skin (as with fair-warm skin)

## Hair Color for Olive Skin (Neutral/Greenish Undertones)

- **Best:** Warm brunette (Kim Kardashian), Deep caramel (Zendaya), Golden balayage (Shay Mitchell), Rich auburn (Salma Hayek)
- **Avoid:** Too-light blondes, overly cool tones that clash with the natural warmth in olive skin

## Hair Color for Dark Skin (Cool Undertones)

- **Best:** Deep espresso brown (Lupita Nyong'o), Cool black (Kerry Washington), Burgundy (Rihanna in deep red tones), Dark blue-black (Naomi Campbell)
- **Avoid:** Brassy blondes, overly warm tones

## Hair Color for Dark Skin (Warm Undertones)

- **Best:** Honey brown (Ciara), Golden caramel (Halle Berry), Chestnut brown (Kelly Rowland), Warm auburn (Tyra Banks)
- **Avoid:** Overly ashy shades that can make the skin look dull

## Universal Hair Colors (Work on Most Skin Tones)

- Rich chocolate brown (Meghan Markle)
- Soft balayage with caramel tones (Jessica Alba)

- Natural black (Zoë Kravitz)
- Warm dark blonde (Gisele Bündchen)

**Eye Color**

Here's a brief guide to what complements these eye colors (both in terms of hair color and in clothes and fashion choices).

BLUE EYES pair beautifully with both warm and cool tones:

- **Cool Tones:** Ash blonde, platinum, silver, cool brown, icy brown, jet-black
- **Warm Tones:** Golden blonde, caramel, honey, copper, warm auburn
- **Bold Choices:** Pastel shades (lavender, baby blue), rich burgundy, midnight blue

GREEN EYES pop with rich, warm tones and earthy shades:

- **Cool Tones:** Ash blonde, cool brown, espresso, dark brown
- **Warm Tones:** Copper, auburn, chestnut, golden blonde, caramel
- **Bold Choices:** Deep reds, jewel-toned greens, soft purples

HAZEL EYES change with light, so they work with many shades:

- **Cool Tones:** Ash blonde, mushroom brown, dark espresso
- **Warm Tones:** Caramel, honey blonde, golden brown, chestnut, rich auburn
- **Bold Choices:** Bronze, deep reds, multidimensional balayage

BROWN EYES are super versatile and
work with nearly any shade:

- **Cool Tones:** Ash brown, cool black, espresso, icy blonde
- **Warm Tones:** Golden brown, caramel, honey blonde, chocolate brown, auburn
- **Bold Choices:** Dark cherry, deep violet, blue-black

GRAY EYES have a unique ability to reflect
color, so they pair well with:

- **Cool Tones:** Platinum blonde, silver, ash brown, charcoal black
- **Warm Tones:** Soft beige blonde, muted copper, warm taupe
- **Bold Choices:** Smoky lilac, icy blue, deep navy

## WHY YOUR HAIR SHOULD BE THE FIRST THING YOU'RE BRAVE ABOUT

My daughter, Kitty-Blu, has always had a fierce spirit. Even when she was little, sitting cross-legged on the bathroom counter while I combed through her tangled hair, she had this quiet confidence—like she knew she was made for more. Back then, it was all about ponytails, messy buns, and "Can you make me look like Ariana today?"

But something changed the year she turned seventeen.

She was about to leave everything she knew behind—our home, her friends, and more importantly, the bullies at school who tried to shrink her light. She was moving to America, starting fresh. And just before she left, she came to me and said, "Dad . . . I want to go blonde."

Now, if you're a hairdresser, you know going blonde is no small decision. It's a big transformation, inside and out. It's a statement. And that's exactly what this was—Kitty-Blu's moment to take control of her identity, to shed her childhood and step into who she was becoming as a young woman.

We lightened her hair slowly and carefully, section by section. As her roots lifted, so did something deeper—her self-belief. Her confidence. Her sense of freedom. When I finished toning and styling, she looked in the mirror with the biggest smile—not just because she loved the blonde, but because she saw herself differently—and she liked what she saw.

I've always told Kitty-Blu that hair is a mirror of your energy. You change your hair when you're ready to change your life—and protect it like you would your peace. Your look should evolve with your spirit, and how you wear your hair should match how you feel about yourself. Don't be afraid to grow, to shed, to start fresh. Ever.

That day, I taught Kitty-Blu that blonde isn't just a color. It's a mindset, not a reductive stereotype, but one that requires courage, maintenance, and commitment. Blondes are powerful as well as fun. Going platinum will draw attention, so be prepared.

Kitty-Blu left for America not as a scared teenager but as a young woman who had taken her power back, with icy blonde hair that said, "This is me now."

What great hair can do for your mental and emotional state is amazing. Being able to dilute insecurities, anxieties, and fears by infusing confidence, beauty, and faith is potent.

# 20.

# It's All About Alignment

### Creating Your Individual Style and
### Image to Match Your Personality

I n a culture full of curated content, aspirational influencers, and endless comparison loops, it's easier than ever to look like *someone*. Or rather, someone else. But looking like *yourself*? That's strangely become harder.

The fact is, real style isn't about chasing trends or copying celebrities. It's not about imitation; it's about *alignment*.

I know from experience that trying to embody the wrong aesthetic can feel like you're wearing a costume. But the right one feels like power. When you match your aesthetic to your personality, your life changes. Not because of vanity, not because of ego. It's because your outside is finally speaking the same language as your inside. You're in alignment, and alignment is magnetic.

I've worked with the most famous faces in the world, icons who live under the brightest lights. But no matter who you are, whether you're getting ready for the Met Gala or your Monday morning meeting, the question is the same: *Does your look reflect your truth?*

I've met many people—especially women—who have curated a look for approval, not alignment. They've chosen "safe" over "*soulful.*" They've spent years trying on someone else's idea of beauty, wearing clothes that don't quite fit their vibe, playing by someone else's rules and style guide, only to wake up one day and realize they feel like strangers in their bodies.

You have to ask yourself: *Are you showing up in your life as the person you are, or who you think you're supposed to be?*

In Part I, I wrote about what you say about yourself without opening your mouth, and how you are both the message and the messenger. Our question then was: *What are those things about your energy and style saying about you?*

Now the question is, more importantly, *is it true?*

Your image isn't just decoration. It's direction.

When you align your outside with your inside, things click into place. You stop second-guessing yourself. You stop chasing trends that were never meant for you. You start moving with purpose, dressing with clarity, and showing up with energy.

And I promise you—people *feel* that.

It's one of my favorite things to see my clients start attracting what matches them—not just compliments (though who doesn't love those?), but connections, respect, and love. Because now, they're leading with *truth*.

You stop shrinking. You start choosing.

When your outside starts telling the truth about your inside, everything around you shifts. People respond to you differently. Opportunities feel like they show up on time instead of passing you by. That's not a coincidence. That's resonance.

That's where confidence meets intention, and that changes *everything*.

It doesn't matter if you're twenty-one and still figuring it all out or fifty-one and ready for your next chapter—your look should evolve with your inner journey. It should *reflect* you. You deserve to take up space in a way that feels authentic, powerful, and beautiful.

I once worked with a woman in her midforties. She was brilliant and wildly talented, but her style was outdated and unflattering. After a big career pivot, where she left the freelance world and went to work for a big reputable company she'd always dreamed of, she came in for a haircut. "I just want something manageable," she said. "All my time has to go toward this job."

"Manageable?" I repeated. "Right now is when you set the stage for your next chapter. Why would you keep yourself small while your life is trying to grow? Grow with it."

She let this sink in. We had a long conversation—not about trends, face shapes, or what was "in," but about who she was becoming with this significant life shift. And once she started speaking from *that* place? The entire vision changed.

I gave her a bold cut. Soft, sculpted layers. A shape with presence. A look that said, *I know who I am now.* And when she saw her reflection, she didn't say, "That looks nice."

She said: "That looks like me. That's me. I look like me."

And here's what happened over the next year:

She got fast-tracked for a role at the streaming network she thought was out of her league.

She started dating again—on her terms, which meant moving off the apps, into actual phone or FaceTime conversations, and then into person for a daytime coffee date.

She showed up to her life, finally, as herself—a woman with her intention, purpose, and energy in alignment.

That's the power of something beyond just a simple haircut—it's the power of alignment.

Finding your personal style that aligns with your aesthetic is more about *curiosity* than commitment. It's about trying things, and then noticing and listening to how those things feel in your body.

I want you to take a minute and really consider these two questions:

**Who are you when no one's watching?**

**What energies, styles, and aesthetics are you drawn to when you're not trying to impress?**

Now, take those answers and get more specific:

**What makes you feel powerful and stand taller?**

**What colors bring your energy forward?**

**What's the last style or outfit that made you feel seen, not just looked at?**

You can wear black head-to-toe and be radiant. You can wear florals and soft waves and be the sharpest person in the office. You can wear streetwear, a structured blazer, or a red lip at 10:00 a.m. if it feels like *you*.

The point isn't the look—it's the *permission*. The most striking people in any room are the ones whose energy matches their aesthetic. Whose hair, clothes, presence—it all sings the same song. They're not performing. They're aligned.

And here's the thing: when you align with your identity, you also attract things that are aligned.

This means more than what's hanging in your closet or how you style your hair. This is about your career. Your friendships.

Your daily habits. When your aesthetic and personality speak the same language, you trust yourself more and need validation less. You stop needing everyone else's opinion to make decisions. You stop asking, *"Is this okay?"* and start asking, *"Is this me?"*

And that shift? That's where everything opens up.

If you've been editing yourself to stay likable or palatable while you wait around for permission to evolve . . . Here is your permission.

When you look in the mirror, does what you see reflect who you really are? Or is your reflection something else? Is it something you've settled for or pretended to be?

If the answer makes you a little uncomfortable, there are adjustments to be made.

Get curious. Try something new. Cut the hair. Change the part. Buy the lipstick. Toss the clothes that never felt right to begin with. Permit yourself space to evolve—not just physically and aesthetically, but energetically.

Once your style and soul start to cohere, you won't just *look* different; you'll *move, lead, and live differently.* I can't repeat it enough, because the stakes are really that high.

And the world will respond to that because you'll finally be showing up as the one person you were always meant to be: *Yourself.*

## QUICK SHOTS AND ACTIONS FOR A MORE STYLISH YOU
### Know Your Vibe Before Choosing Your Style

What energy do I want to bring into the room? Return to chapter three when we walked through a few examples about what your brand has the potential to say about you. Are you polished and professional? Effortlessly cool? Wild and unpredictable? Soft and romantic? Bold and high fashion?

You don't need to pick one forever, but knowing your *current* vibe helps you cut through the noise and make intentional choices.

*Action Step:* Make a quick "mood board" album on your phone with 10–15 images that feel like *you*. Not who you think you should be. Who you *are* or who you're becoming. That's your visual compass.

## Choose a Cut That Matches Your Confidence Level

Hair is energy. It can weigh you down or lift you. Think of your haircut as a *visual name tag*. What are possible messages that your haircut is saying?

- Long, heavy, unlayered hair = safety net
- Structured, shaped hair = intention
- Face-framing = openness
- Sharp cuts = boldness
- Soft texture = ease and fluidity

*Action Step:* Next time you're in the chair, ask your stylist: "What shape would make me feel more powerful?" instead of "What's trending?" Power over popularity—always. Start asking yourself: "What version of myself am I ready to be seen as?" Let the color amplify that mood.

## Polish Isn't About Perfection. It's About Intention.

Looking "put together" isn't about spending hours on a look. It's about *consistency and curation*. A great blow-dry isn't just for red carpets. Clean ends, healthy shine, and structure make people take you seriously. You don't have to do the most, just learn how to do the basics *well*.

*Action Step:* Master one go-to polished look. Whether it's a sleek ponytail, a bouncy wave, or a clean middle part, master that look so it feels easy. Confidence comes from *knowing* you look good.

### Dress the Part of the Life You Want

Your outfit, hair, makeup, or grooming should all be in the *same conversation*.

Mismatch = mixed signals

Alignment = magnetism

*Action Step*: Choose three words you want your *whole look* to say daily. Examples:

- Confident. Clean. Effortless.
- Playful. Edgy. Free.
- Elegant. Structured. Glam.

Before you leave the house, do a quick check. "Do my hair, outfit, and energy reflect those three words?" If not, adjust. You're the stylist now.

### Don't Just Copy—Customize.

Inspiration is everywhere, but replication rarely works. What works for a celebrity might not work for you. That's not a failure. That's freedom. Everything should be put through your filter so that it suits and enhances you. You don't want to be the person wearing someone else's costume or personality.

*Action Step:* If you bring in a reference photo (please do!), ask your stylist: "What about this look could work *for me?*"

Make it a collaboration, not a cosplay.

**Routine = Power. Ritual = Presence.**

You don't need a 10-step hair regimen. But you *do* need a system. A simple, thoughtful routine creates consistency. Consistency builds confidence.

*Action Step:* Lock in your basics. For example:

- A solid shampoo + conditioner that works for your texture
- A heat protectant (*nonnegotiable*)
- A go-to finishing product that brings the shine, shape, or structure

Then, *use them* with intention. That's how you polish your energy, not just your hair.

When your aesthetic reflects your personality, the world responds differently. You stop trying to fit in and begin to stand out. You attract what *matches* you. Your job isn't to look like anyone else, it's to be so fully *you* that there's no room for confusion.

That's the kind of beauty that doesn't fade.


## LESSONS FROM LEGENDS

Style isn't just about aesthetics—it's a language.

It speaks long before you do. It introduces you. It reflects you. And if you're not careful, it can define you before you've even had a chance to.

The legends—the ones who shifted culture, not just followed trends—have always understood this. From platinum blonde bombshells to androgynous icons, they didn't just dress up. They showed up. Loudly, softly, intentionally. Their hair wasn't just hair. It was punctuation. Personality. Power.

## Marilyn Monroe: The Power of Soft Glamour

Marilyn didn't stumble into her look—she chose it. Bleaching her hair was more than a beauty move; it was a declaration. Norma Jeane became Marilyn when she rewrote her story in waves of platinum blonde. But it wasn't just about allure—it was strategy. Her image became a shield, a weapon, a seduction, a mask. She reminds us that style can be both liberation and illusion—and asks the question: Are you crafting your look for validation, or are you owning it for yourself?

## Elvis Presley: Rebellion in a Pompadour

Elvis's jet-black pompadour was the epitome of controlled chaos. It wasn't accidental—it was a challenge to the clean-cut mold of the '50s. He injected swagger into conformity and turned his hair into a cultural reset. It wasn't just style. It was signal. He reminds us: sometimes, breaking the rules starts with how you wear your hair.

## Audrey Hepburn: Simplicity as Strength

Audrey didn't need theatrics. Her pixie cut, paired with doe eyes and quiet strength, stripped beauty down to its bones—and made it iconic. At a time when bigger was better, she went minimal and made maximum impact. Her look whispered, but it landed like thunder. A reminder: real elegance isn't loud—it's deliberate.

## Madonna: Reinvention as Power

No one has used hair as a weapon of reinvention like Madonna. She flipped the script and disrupted culture over and over—punk bleach, spiritual reds, Hollywood waves. With every transformation, she was both challenging and reclaiming identity, conceptually. Madonna showed us that change isn't weakness—it's evolution. She didn't follow trends—she created eras. And when the world got too comfortable, Madonna changed again.

## Tilda Swinton: Androgyny as Art

Tilda doesn't wear a look. She inhabits it. Every cut, color, and texture she chooses is a statement. She moves between silver crops and sculptural shapes like a living canvas. Her aesthetic isn't about vanity—it's about vision. And in her mystery, we find magnetism. She shows us: to be unforgettable, you don't need to fit the mold—you need to melt it.

## Kim Kardashian: Curation as Currency

Kim's hair lives in constant, camera-ready perfection—glass-straight obsidian, platinum drama, soft waves with razor-sharp center parts. Nothing is random. Nothing is accidental. Every look is crafted with clockwork precision, designed to dominate feeds and fuel fashion trends. She's turned curation into capital. A living billboard for how visual narrative is powerful. Kim proves: when you know your brand, you can shape the world to match it.

## Zendaya: The Chameleon with Purpose

Zendaya's style is the blueprint for modern transformation. One moment she's old-Hollywood glam, the next she's futuristic and fierce. She moves fluidly—but never loses her core. Her hair reflects her generation: adaptive, bold, and unboxed. She shows us: you don't have to stick to one identity—you just have to own each one fully.

### Erykah Badu: Sacred Style

Erykah doesn't wear fashion—she channels it. Her hair is culture, heritage, and spiritual expression. From massive headwraps to braided crowns, her style honors ancestry while pushing artistry. She teaches us: your roots are your crown.

## WHAT ABOUT YOU?

What's your Image?

What are you really saying when you walk into a room?

Are you blending in—or standing in your truth? Are you styling out of habit—or out of intention?

When you own your image, you're not just putting on a look. You're putting out a message. You're showing the world how to treat you, how to read you—and how to remember you.

The next time you adjust your hair in the mirror, ask:

What do I want to say today?

What do I want the world to see?

Because when style speaks with purpose . . .
People don't just see you.
They feel you.

# PART IV

# PROTECTING AND PRESERVING YOUR GROWTH

# 21.

# Developing Layers Beneath the Surface

*The Unsung Heroes of Your Personal Growth*

Layers can transform a basic, lifeless haircut into something with movement, depth, and dimension. If you've had a haircut more than once, you've probably gotten layers and seen the difference that their structure and support can make. Our personal growth, which makes you the complicated, multidimensional human that you are, is also developed by layers.

Every challenge, realization, and learning moment, especially our mistakes, adds another layer. Most people probably don't even recognize that they've been under construction their whole life.

But where you're standing today? You are the culmination of the layers you've developed.

This also means that the person you were last year differs from the one you'll be next year. As you evolve, you continue to grow existing layers and add new ones. Your personal development is an ongoing process until the day you die. So why not focus on developing the layers that lift and better your life rather than reinforcing the ones that keep dragging you down?

In every layer lies an opportunity.

## THE BASE LAYER

The first and most crucial layer that you tend to is your foundation: self-awareness. The rest of the structure is questionable at best if this layer is a mess.

Who *are* you? What makes you tick? What are your values, and what is the standard by which you live your life? Do you know what you actually like? Do you have your own opinions and points of view? Or do you repeat what you hear or have been told by others without investigation? In everything from shopping to conversations with friends, I always try to be vigilant about asking myself this question: "Is this my opinion, or am I just repeating something I know will make me appear a certain way? What do *I* believe?"

This goes back to what you read about examining your roots and finding what is yours by choice, not inheritance or osmosis. Adopting the point of view of someone you admire or trust isn't the same as having your own. You're effectively training your brain to run all of your opinions by something external—so when you sit out of making your own choices, you are relinquishing your voice and identity.

That is not growth. That's laziness or cowardice, and that's not who you are.

The truth is, personal growth isn't just about collecting good vibes and surviving the grind. It's about knowing yourself intimately enough to identify underdeveloped areas of your life and those holding you back.

This is where you get brutally honest because you love yourself. What is genuine, and what is ego or image management? Who are you? Think past ideas like, *I'm a people pleaser or I'm a morning person.* Those are not who you are. They're sound bites. You need to know who you are deep down, what you want, how you feel, and why you do what you do, unequivocally, to develop the layers that will improve your life.

Truly, it's a thrill to deeply understand yourself, know your core beliefs and what feels right in your body, and *then* ACT from that place of certainty.

## THE FRIENDSHIP LAYER

You walk through your life with the friendships you make. While some people keep the same three friends they've had since childhood, most find that their friends change as their lives do. School friends get replaced by your friends at university or by work friends. When you're in a relationship, maybe you transition to couple friends, and then when you have kids, you become friends with their friends' parents. The cycle continues to change throughout life and each of its phases.

As you reflect on your relationships, I want you to remember the question I asked in Section III: Which people in your life are bringing you real growth and nourishing your potential? Identify these people clearly. Just like hair requires regular maintenance, so do friendships.

Make a list of the relationships in your life that leave you feeling energized, challenged in a healthy way, never judged, and truly seen. If you're like I was years ago, and have no one that immediately comes to mind, make the commitment to give those things to *the relationship that you have with yourself*—it's tied to what you end up tolerating (in yourself and your friendships).

Which friendships in your life are worth pouring your time and energy into? It's time to let go, or set boundaries, with any connections that drain and drag you down and stall your personal progress. As you develop your friendship layers, you'll find freedom from the fact that not every friendship is meant to last forever. Some are seasonal or will be with you for only part of your journey. When you constantly evolve and change, you might find that distant history is the only thing you have in common with certain people. All that's connecting you is that you've known them for a long time.

These things are helpful to remember as you consider why you're investing in certain friendships—and whether these friends-by-association are taking up space that could be devoted to other people.

Have you ever looked at a friend and thought, *How are we still friends?* It's no different than looking at a picture of yourself ten years ago with a hideous hairstyle and thinking, *Why did no one stop me? How could I not see this was bad?*

Friendship isn't one big thing; it's a million little things and moments. There's every possibility that you can outgrow friendships when you grow in different directions and develop different layers. Friendships are like roots; some lift you, and others pull you down.

Then you have some friendships (and relationships) turn toxic. In the simplest terms, they stop being good for you.

When you think about your friendships, can you recognize who in your circle adds value to your life? People who are easy to connect with, listen, share some of the same values and interests, show up when you need them, and most importantly, make your life better.

Who are your most supportive friends? Who are you the best version of a friend to? Those are the relationships that feed your growth and should get your energy.

Who are the people you feel drained by? Are there friends you feel like you're always the only one putting in effort? Are there friends that, every time they text you, you feel dread rather than joy?

Developing your friendship layer can sometimes mean losing friendships you've outgrown or which have become a source of difficulty that is no longer reasonable.

## THE FAMILY LAYER

The family layer changes significantly during life because your position in it evolves, and the shape of your family expands and contracts. Marriages, divorces, births, and deaths reconfigure your family's size, roles, and maturity.

You are initially the dependent child in your family of origin, but the dynamics and relationships shift over the following decades. You become an independent adult, no longer under the care and supervision of your parents. You don't need them like you used to, and that adjustment doesn't always go smoothly.

The growing pains are part and parcel of developing your family layers. Your family, those who raised you, give you the tools to navigate your other relationships. These tools might be top-of-the-line, shiny, and new, or they might be rusty and fucked-up.

Not everyone is equipped with the same tools in their family layer. Circling back to the part of this book that had you examine your roots, you can probably recognize the helpful and damaging tools used on and given to you.

I shared earlier how neither of my parents had parents who lived past their early childhood, so they had virtually no tools other than the ones they forged themselves when raising my siblings and me.

Breaking away from your role in your family when you were younger is metaphorically like dying your hair pink and piercing your nose. You are claiming yourself in a new way. Something you will do numerous times as you develop your layers.

As you become involved in romantic entanglements or possibly get married, you bring someone new into your family's fold. Not everyone will understand or be happy for you. Suddenly, you can find your allegiance torn between your family of origin and your partner, your chosen family.

It's complicated to get caught between all these expectations when your family demands your obedience, but your partner demands your devotion and loyalty. For those who raised you, you are still their child; seeing you in other lights doesn't come easily—and remember to give them empathy for that.

Also remember that no familial roles stay the same forever. If you get married, your family, including your spouse and their family, grows further; your siblings may get married and take some attention off you and your spouse, etc. If you or they have children, these dynamics will shift even more with your family of origin and your extended family, and it's not always without hurt feelings and bruised egos.

Developing the family layer that works for *your* family unit is pivotal, with you and your partner at the head. Finding ways to compromise or communicate about all these expectations is just another facet of your ongoing personal growth in this layer.

## THE CAREER LAYER

At some point, you must ask yourself the big question: *What are you doing with your life?*

You didn't think I was going to go there, did you? Make no mistake, I am casting no judgment about your line of work or career track. But keeping with the idea of living intentionally, what you do with your life should have a focused trajectory— and perhaps even be fun.

Ask yourself, is your job still giving you any sense of purpose? Or are you just collecting a paycheck and hoping the weekend arrives soon enough to forget about it? If so, is there any work you're doing outside of your job that *does* give you purpose?

This is where your career gets layered in, and you add more depth to your life. Your job doesn't have to be climbing the corporate ladder; it's what you want to do with your time, so it feels additive to your life. At the very least, it should be engaging your strengths and exploiting what is unique to you.

Sometimes, you need to cut out the "dead ends" of your professional life. It's easy to get stuck in a rut or be too afraid to pivot and do something completely different. But developing your professional layers is about finding that part of the Venn diagram that holds the cross section of what excites you and how you can earn a living.

Ask yourself if you'd still do your job if money weren't a factor. This isn't a trick question. It's an insightful question. If the answer is no, maybe it's time to rethink things. What do you want to do, and what actions can you take to move onto that career path? And if you don't know what it is that you want, tap back into your envy. Who has your dream job? What career do you see that you think you'd be great at?

The signs are all around you.

If you don't work for whatever reason (and I do not consider child rearing as "not working" because that is an important job)—then think of your career layer as your altruistic layer. What can you do with your time to be of service? How can you contribute to your community or important causes with your time and talents?

Having purpose and being of service is a meaningful experience in life. Purpose and service enrich you as much, if not more, than those you serve.


## THE EMOTIONAL LAYER

Your emotional layer is the most fragile. It's the delicate, wispy layer that, despite the impression we want to give people, can be blown apart instantly. Even the strongest, most stable person you know gets their emotions rocked, especially by some of the aforementioned family, friends, and career layers.

Your emotional intelligence develops with emotional growth; sometimes, the growth isn't pretty. It takes addressing past traumas, getting comfortable with your vulnerabilities, and processing your disappointments with solutions or actions rather than letting them derail you.

I firmly believe in feeling your feelings for as long as necessary. I'm not advocating for stuffing everything inside. It's better to feel things for too long than not allow yourself to feel at all.

Even more than feeling them, I believe in understanding your emotions when they hit you rather than spinning out. When I get rocked by an unexpected emotion, whether in a surprising situation, event, or occurrence, I pause and take a deep breath. Instead of habitually reacting or immediately spiraling, which I used to do, I've gotten in the practice of asking myself, "What am I feeling? How can I process this? What is deregulating me? What is my next step?"

I don't have to react immediately; I can give myself a beat and be present with my emotions. I'm not missing any opportunities by not responding right away. Understanding the correct size and scope of what is happening and how I feel helps me emotionally regulate and react accordingly.

I don't like feeling out of control with my emotions for several reasons, the most important being that I never want to be someone others are afraid to share things with. I know that being able to regulate myself emotionally makes me a safe person for those I care for the most. My children and friends don't feel responsible for my feelings or worry about my ability to manage them when they come to me with anything.

It's easy to overreact reflexively when your emotions are suddenly activated. It happens so quickly. You can find yourself assigning motivation or intent that may not be there, and you want to act on the heat that you're feeling. Developing your emotional layer will make you happier because you have more stability and control. It will also grow your emotional intelligence, which will serve you in every aspect of your life.

## THE PHYSICAL AND MENTAL
## HEALTH LAYERS

Your physical and mental well-being are the health layers that, paired with your emotions, set the tone for everything in your life. If you are unhealthy in your body, mind, and spirit, everything else will suffer.

It sounds obvious because it is, but you still probably don't do what you know is required to keep yourself healthy. I know this about you because I am guilty of the same.

I don't drink enough water daily, sleep enough hours, and always eat food that will fuel my body rather than slow me down or make me feel gluttonous or guilty. I also don't avoid screens hours before bedtime or peel my eyes away from my phone and social media when it's making me feel anxious, insecure, or hostile toward myself.

And I feel the effects. I can still function, but I am not at my best.

You're lucky if you get through your lifetime without significant blows to your body or mind. When you look at the statistics, you see how prevalent disease and illness are. After two-plus years of the COVID pandemic, we've collectively grown more conscious that our health should be protected at all costs.

Addressing your physical health layer means yearly checkups, physical exercise, prioritizing your health, and doing everything possible to prevent issues. That would be getting enough sleep, paying attention to nutrition, exercising regularly, understanding your bloodwork, understanding your body's needs, and not hiding from the reality of your weaknesses. Are these integrated into your mental health life or are they afterthoughts?

Your mental health needs as much attention as your physical and emotional health. Anxiety and depression are common parts of life. The stress of just existing in this time has wreaked havoc on our mental states. Anxiety, depression, OCD, bipolar disorder, and mental health issues can be managed with therapy and/or life-changing medication if properly diagnosed.

There is no stigma attached to asking for and receiving help. I've struggled with crippling anxiety all my life, and only because of the help of my therapist have I been able to manage it. If you're struggling with mental health issues, seek help. You don't have to suffer.

Love-based relationships boost mental health, so frequently connect with your friends and family. If you can't have FaceTime or a phone call, send a text or a meme—digital connection is a form of love. Meditation and tapping into your faith also boost mental health, so download an app to quiet your mind and fill your heart. Music is a source of serotonin and dopamine. Listen to the songs that lift you up. Make yourself a great playlist for when you're feeling down or out of sorts.

## THE SELF-ACCEPTANCE LAYER

The last and one of the most crucial layers of personal growth is your self-acceptance layer. That's when you stop apologizing for being you and accept yourself exactly where you are in this current moment. There is no such thing as being perfect; there is only being you. Your layers, the ones you are working to develop further, come together in a unique, beautiful, perfectly imperfect way.

Personal growth is like messy, layered hair. It takes time to shape and get it right. The best news is that until you take your last breath, you are never "done." Every layer you develop adds more depth, texture, and personality.

Keep developing them, building the better you, trimming away what stunts your growth, and don't forget to look in the mirror and appreciate how hard you work and how hot you look.

Your layers are the only validation you need.

A new client came into my studio on January 4th. Her hair was tied in a low, loose bun. You could tell it hadn't been brushed in days—maybe even weeks. I've learned not to take that personally. It's not about the hair. It's about what the hair reveals.

When she took the elastic out, the whole picture came into focus.

Her hair was brittle. Jagged in places. Dark in some parts, brassy in others—like it couldn't decide what it was trying to be. There were even chunks where you could see she'd tried to cut it herself, probably late at night, with dull scissors and either too many thoughts or too much alcohol.

She laughed as it fell over her shoulders. "I know," she said, waving a hand over the chaos. "It's a metaphor."

I smiled. "That bad, huh?"

"Yeah," she said. "My hair and I have been through it."

"Rough New Year's Eve?"

"You could say that."

I stayed silent, knowing that if I did, she would continue talking.

She told me she'd been making fast choices lately to see where life took her. Whether it was cycling through new friendships, bouncing from job to job, or always making sure that she had plans, there was no substance because everything had become surface level. And no peace because she had zero time to reflect. Chaos had become the baseline for emotional comfort. Her choices weren't grounded in instinct or insight; they were driven by impulse.

I told her it sounded like she was grabbing at things in her life because they were there, not because they were right.

"I thought I was being spontaneous," she said. "But I'm finding out you can't build a life on impulsive behavior and shortcuts."

I've seen it before in hair and people. The damage doesn't always come from one big mistake. Sometimes, it's just a series of little mistakes stacked on each other and left untended until one day, you wake up and realize everything is worse than you thought. This is when you become *scattered* instead of *layered*.

"Okay," I said. "It's a new year. The perfect time to start over and build it right. One layer at a time."

I began with a soft reset, cleaning up the ends and removing the uneven weight. Slowly, I started designing the structure—not just the shape but the support layers that would frame her face, lift her eyes, and give her movement without all the chaos. Layers that weren't just stacked but belonged to one another and built on each other with intention.

I used a dry-cutting technique to see exactly how the hair moved, reacted, and curved. That's the thing about real growth: you can't force it into place. You work *with* the hair, guide it gently, and respect the texture.

As we worked, I talked to her about layers.

"This is the self-awareness layer," I said, pointing to the shortest pieces around her face. "It's where you see yourself."

"These," I said, carving gentle layers through the mid-lengths, "are your friendship and family layers. They sit close to your core and help shape how you feel. They're soft but supportive."

Then I motioned to the longer, foundational pieces underneath—the ones that hold everything else up. "This is your career or purpose layer. It doesn't need to be flashy, but it needs to be *solid*. You build on it. And you protect it."

She laughed. "What about the frizzy, fried parts?"

"That's your mental health layer. And we don't fix that with a flat iron. We fix it by really tending to it, by not ignoring it anymore."

She went quiet, but I saw it in her eyes when it clicked.

Hair, like life, can't be rushed, but it can be repaired. You can't deep-condition your way out of your problems or your burnout. You need to go back, find the weak points, and re-build with patience, layer by layer.

When I finished the cut, her hair looked like it belonged to her. It framed, supported, and moved with her. It had intention.

She ran her hands through it slowly. "I feel . . . good. Grounded. More rooted and balanced."

"I think this is going to be your year." I winked at her in the mirror.

"I do, too."

Sometimes you catch someone in the perfect moment where they can listen to what they need to hear. This was one of those days.

## 22.

# Listen to the Right Voices
# and Silence All the Rest

### *The Only Ones That Matter
### Are the Ones on Team You*

By thirteen, I had already figured out one thing—I loved transformation. I loved watching it in shows on television and seeing how heroes, villains, and romantic leads would change their looks with their story arcs. I was transfixed by how a certain style could transform how someone looked and carried themselves. I wanted to be a part of that.

I didn't know other people my age who felt this way, but I didn't care. I got my hands on anyone who would let me, convincing them to let me restyle, shape, or even experiment with their hair—my sisters, my friends, my mum. I would constantly try new things, making them a Hollywood siren one day and a new wave pop star the next.

Mum was the first to see where this could go. Once, as I was fixing my sister's hair in the kitchen, she said, "You know, you should do this properly. You should work in a salon."

It hadn't occurred to me that working in a salon was something I could do. It seemed like such a grown-up thing—having a job other than mowing lawns, shoveling snow, or delivering papers. I didn't even know anyone my age who worked indoors.

But once those words spilled out of my mum's mouth, it was all I could think about. She voiced a belief in me, and suddenly my small life felt filled with possibility.

There was a salon in town that I knew was the real deal. Busy, professional, the kind of place where people left looking like they owned the world. I needed to be in that environment. There was only one problem—I was thirteen. Too young to get a job. But I was tall for my age, I had confidence, and a good poker face. Sometimes that's all it takes.

So, I lied.

I walked in, asked for a job, and told them what I could offer: a good work ethic, an insight into youth culture and trends, and my self-taught hairdressing skills. When they asked my age, I told them I was fifteen. I half expected them to laugh me out the door.

Instead, they gave me a trial.

It wasn't exactly what I imagined. I wasn't cutting hair, I wasn't holding scissors, and I definitely wasn't transforming anyone yet. I was cleaning, running errands, and making coffee just how the stylists liked it. Ten-hour shifts for £1 an hour, after long bus rides from school. But I didn't care.

Even though I wasn't behind the chair, I was watching and learning. I was in an environment that felt right in my body. I felt a sense of safety and inclusion that I hadn't experienced at school or with my peers. I was where the action was. It was another voice affirming that I was in the right place.

I remember standing off to the side on my first day, trying to keep out of the way while taking everything in. The smell of fresh dye, the sound of blow-dryers, and the conversations flowing from every station. But more than anything, I noticed the shift between when someone came in and when they left.

A woman would walk in, eyes down, hair scraped back, barely acknowledging herself in the mirror. Then, after an hour in the chair—whether it was a fresh cut, a color, or a style—she'd leave looking alive. Back straight, head high. She'd catch a glimpse of herself in the window as she walked out, as if she almost didn't recognize the confidence staring back at her.

Being a hairdresser isn't just cutting hair or just a job at all. It's a service that goes so much deeper than that.

At school, I was still stuck in a place that didn't fit—still dealing with people who didn't get me. But in the salon, I had a purpose. I had direction.

The moment I turned sixteen, I left school and started working full-time. I wanted to be on the stylist floor as soon as possible. I studied every cut, technique, and trick I could pick up from the experienced stylists around me.

And something changed in me, too.

For years, dyslexia had made reading and writing a constant struggle. Written work felt impossible, like I was constantly fighting against something I couldn't control. But when it came to hair? The words made sense. The theory, the techniques, the textbooks I had to read, and even the essays for my hairdressing NVQ 1, 2 & 3 and my L'Oréal Color Degree—I could do them, because I wanted to. Passion outweighed the struggle. It's amazing what you're able to work through when you want something.

Hairdressing wasn't just a way out. It was a way through.

I had spent so much of my life feeling boxed in, waiting for the moment I could prove who I really was. And now, for the first time, I knew exactly where I belonged.

My hunger for hair wasn't fading—it grew, rapidly. And for

some reason, it wasn't enough just to be good. I had to be the best. Maybe I had something to prove; perhaps it was a way to silence the doubt that had followed me for years, or maybe it was just the fire inside me that wouldn't settle for anything less.

I became obsessed. I watched everyone around me, every stylist whose work I felt inspired by. I studied their hands, their movements, the way they approached hair like it was a living thing, something to be shaped and brought to life. I was a sponge, soaking in every bit of knowledge I could. Every spare moment I had, I worked. Every client was another opportunity to perfect my craft. And it paid off.

I worked my way up the salon's price scale faster than most. At first, I was just assisting, learning, and proving myself. Then, I was taking on my own clients. Before I knew it, I had my own price scale, my own name on the books, and my own clients asking for me.

But I wanted more.

I started looking beyond the salon, beyond the day-to-day haircuts and color jobs. That's when I discovered the world of editorial hair.

This was another level entirely. It wasn't just about making people feel good—it was about creativity, pushing boundaries, and setting trends rather than following them. Editorial hair meant working on magazine shoots, runway shows, and backstage at Fashion Week. It was the place where hair became art. And I wanted in.

The voices said, "Yes, you're on to something. That's where you're meant to go."

I took the first step. I built a portfolio—photo after photo of my work, proof that I could create something beyond the everyday. And then, with nothing but my ambition and a dream, I left Leicester and took it to London.

I knocked on doors, walked into agencies, and showed my portfolio to anyone who would look. Most of the time, I got nothing. A polite nod, a "We'll be in touch," and then silence. But I didn't stop. I kept showing up. I kept pushing.

And eventually, someone said yes. I booked a job assisting a more established hairdresser for a photo shoot for a local advertisement.

That was how it started—assisting at fashion shows, getting a glimpse of the world I had only dreamed about. That was how I built a bridge from salon to session stylist. Then I started doing my own shoots, small ones at first, building my name, proving myself.

Then came the moment.

I had done a photoshoot—just another job, another step forward. But this one was different. My work ended up on the cover of *Hairdressers Journal*, an industry magazine. That alone was huge for me. But then something happened that I never expected.

I read an interview with Vidal Sassoon, the biggest name in hair, the legend. In the middle of his conversation with the journalist, he pointed to a magazine cover and said something that stopped me.

"Whoever did the hair on this cover—I love it."

He pointed to the industry magazine for which I had done the cover. I read that line over and over. Sassoon himself had seen my work. And he hadn't just seen it—he liked it.

I sat there, staring at the page, my mind racing. Chris Appleton—the kid from Leicester who had started sweeping floors and lying about his age to get into a salon—had just gotten recognition from Sassoon. It should have been the moment I finally felt like I had made it. But instead, I felt something else.

Imposter syndrome.

It crept in like a whisper, a nagging voice of doubt. Was it a hundred percent for sure the magazine I had done the cover of? Maybe it was a mistake. Maybe he thought someone else had done the hair. Maybe it was just luck.

I thought those insecurities had been silenced long before, but now there they were coming out of hibernation to torment me. Ironically, instead of feeling assurance, I started to question everything. Was I good enough? Had I earned this? All I could hear were the negative voices, and their volume was rising.

I had worked hard and hustled to get the opportunities I got. I had proven my talent and done great work. I was being measured based on my efforts, not anyone else's. Vidal Sassoon's praise should have legitimized me in a way I had never felt before, but instead, it brought up every insecurity I had.

I took a breath and centered myself. I knew I was listening to those voices trying to tear me down, but I struggled in the moment to separate what was fact and what was feeling.

Vidal Sassoon is a legend. He's the most famous, revered, respected, and arguably the best hairdresser in the world. He knows hair. These are facts. So why was I now questioning his opinion as the master of our craft, because I didn't feel my work was worthy of his praise? Did Vidal Sassoon suddenly no longer know hair? OR was I overwhelmed by the moment and defaulting to old ideas, past traumas, and my inner critic? Was I unable to accept this big of a compliment? Those were the feelings wrestling for control in me.

I've struggled with anxiety and self-doubt for much of my life. That doesn't make me unique, but it made me susceptible to the wrong voices when success started coming my way.

I reminded myself how incredible things happen when you listen to the right voice, and in fact, it invites more voices to join the chorus. Vidal Sassoon had just joined my chorus.

As I took time to reflect on this and dissect my inner voices, a feeling of validation replaced my anxiety and insecurity. I belonged in editorial hair styling. I was good enough. I felt inspired to keep going, with Vidal Sassoon urging me on.

Life will find plenty of new and creative ways to tear you down. Listening to the right voices and tuning out the wrong ones took a complete reconditioning for me. It was no easy feat. Growing up, I was so used to the negative voices and opinions of bullies, teachers, peers, and even myself, that for years afterward I struggled to hear the voices of praise, approval, and affirmation.

This ties back to all of the stuff you read about earlier in the book about how you harm yourself with negative self-talk, unrealistic comparisons, and by weaponizing your insecurities.

The right voices tell you to be brave, follow your dreams, ask for what you need, and bring you the accolades you deserve.

The right voices say, "How can I help?"

The right voices aren't in competition with you or trying to win at your expense.

The right voices know there's enough success for everyone and want you to have yours.


I was on an overnight flight from Los Angeles to London last year, and just as I had finished applying my hydrating sheet mask (one of my little flight rituals), my seatmate turned to me and said, "Sorry to bother you, but are you Chris Appleton?"

She was midtwenties, cute, wearing her hair in a sloppy bun, and looking at me intently.

"I am. Should I be afraid?" I teased, feeling a little vulnerable with my sheet mask on, strapped beside her for the next ten hours.

"Can I ask your opinion about something?" she asked politely.

I leaned in, ready for her question, and what she told me was unfortunately not that surprising. She had been growing out her hair for the last two years so she could have long hair for her wedding, which was in four months. I nodded, waiting for the issue to unfold.

Her friends had thrown her a destination bachelorette party in Cabo, and while they were getting ready to go out one night, she and one of her bridesmaids fought. It was a '90s-themed night at the club that they were going to, and her bridesmaid wanted to crimp her hair.

My seatmate explained that she told her bridesmaid she didn't want to damage her hair for a themed club night. She had been taking hair vitamins, avoiding unnecessary heat tools, and even using hair sunscreen so that her hair would be the perfect length and in the best health for her wedding.

Her bridesmaid guilted her, saying that everyone had spent a lot of money to come to her bachelorette weekend, and the least she could do was participate in the festivities. The other brides-maids refused to take sides, opting to stay out of it, but there was a point when everyone was looking at her in awkward silence.

I raised an eyebrow. "I feel like this story is about to take a bad turn."

"Oh, it does." She pulled her hair out of the sloppy bun, and I could see the very clear burn damage.

"So the bridesmaid crimped your hair. And she obviously didn't use a heat protectant spray?"

"No. I'll have the smell of burning hair in my nostrils for-ever."

I asked her, kindly and without judgment, why she let this bridesmaid guilt her like that.

"She's my friend and had arranged this beautiful bachelor-ette trip for me, and I felt like I had to."

"It sounds like you listened to the wrong voices. Not only did you let her manipulate you with guilt, but you also didn't protect what you value most—your wedding day."

"I'm such a fucking people pleaser and now my hair is ruined. What can I do to fix it in the next four months?"

I told her that her hair wasn't ruined; this was a setback, not a disaster. I suggested a few different treatments that would help salvage its condition. Sadly, once your hair is burned, you can undo only so much damage.

But then we got into a longer conversation about the actual situation. I'm a recovering people pleaser, so I know that terrain very well. It's easy to get swept up in what other people think and feel, and sacrifice your own well-being to put their needs above your own. The struggle is so real, and it takes incredible discipline to recognize your people-pleasing ways and stop yourself from doing them.

The more concerning parts were that she wasn't confident enough to stand up for herself to one of her best friends—and that her supposed best friends didn't respect her wishes for such an important day. Obviously, there were long-term friendship dynamics that I wasn't clued in to, but it was clear that ultimately she was giving the wrong people too much volume in her life—those who were pressuring her—and not listening to the right one—her own, which was protecting her.

"Sometimes we accommodate the people in our life because it's easier than if we don't," I said. "But you need to adjust the levels of the voices you listen to, because even your closest friends don't always want what's best for you if it's not best for them, too. Or if it's different than what they want themselves."

She looked at me, surprised. "My friends aren't like that."

"Aren't they, though? Think about the story you just told me. You set a boundary, and your friends pushed or guilted you to cross it for one night at a club in Cabo."

"Well, it was my bachelorette party, not just a night in Cabo," she said defensively.

"Was your night better because you crimped and burned your hair? Did you make better memories with your friends because you conceded and crossed your boundary? Or are you now sitting next to a hairdresser you do not know, asking how to fix the mistake of having conceded?"

She took a breath, clearly processing. "No, we didn't make better memories. I was just pissed off all night because I knew my hair was going to be fucked."

I reassured her. "That's what I thought. It's in there. The voice telling you, 'This doesn't feel right,' or 'I don't want this.' You have to stop listening to the noise around you for a second and hear it."

She and I talked for another hour on the flight, and I gave her my number to keep me posted on how the hair treatments worked. Four months later, she texted me a photo of her wedding day. She looked happy, her hair cascaded into soft curls to her shoulders and looked much healthier than when she unraveled her sloppy bun on the airplane.

Below the photo were the words, "This is me listening to the right voices!"

There's a reason we doubt ourselves even when we *know* better. A reason we hesitate even when the door's wide open. A reason we self-sabotage right when things start getting good.

It's not always because we're afraid of failing; sometimes it's because we've been trained to *listen to the wrong voices.*

The one that told you not to get your hopes up.

The one that made you second-guess your ambition.

The one who scoffed when you shared your dream out loud.

The one that said, "Who do you think you are?"

Sometimes it isn't even that cruel. Sometimes it's wrapped in concern or disguised as "being realistic." But just because a voice sounds familiar—or comes from someone you love—doesn't mean it belongs in your head.

## ADJUSTING THE LEVELS

This exercise is about turning down the volume on the voices that *don't serve you*, and learning how to *amplify the ones that do*.

### Step 1: Tune In to the Loudest Voices Right Now

Take a deep breath. Get quiet. Think about the way you talk to yourself when:

- You're about to make a bold move in your life (fighting for a raise, asking a stranger out).
- You're doubting your next step.
- You've just made a mistake.
- You're getting dressed in front of the mirror.

What are the responses? Are they encouraging? Gentle? Insecure? Practical?

What are the loudest voices I hear in these moments? Whose tone, language, or energy do they remind me of?

Write down the ones that live rent-free in your head. Be specific. You might hear:

- Your dad's voice, reminding you to be practical.
- A former boss, pointing out what you're not doing well enough.

- That frenemy who always made backhanded compliments sound like support.
- An ex who made you feel like too much and not enough simultaneously.
- A teacher who said you were "average."

Write their names or labels. Then, next to each one, write what *message* they keep repeating.

Now ask yourself: Are these voices helping me grow, or keeping me small?

### Step 2: Name the Positive Voices (Even the Quiet Ones)

Now flip the script.

Think back to the moments when you felt the most like yourself—powerful, seen, inspired, capable. Who was in your corner during those moments?

These voices might be quieter. That's normal. Encouragement is often subtle, while criticism shouts. But we're about to fix that.

List the people who *truly* believed in you, even if they didn't say much. It could be:

- A mentor who saw your potential before you did.
- A friend who always listens without casting judgment.
- Your younger self, before life got noisy.
- A stranger who said one kind thing at precisely the right time.

- A future version of you, living the life you're building right now.

Who are yours? Who do you hear?

Consider a negative situation you find yourself in right now—a dilemma, a struggle, an insecurity you're battling. Next to each person, write what they'd say to you *right now*, if you let them speak up.

Then ask: How would my life change if I listened to these voices more?

What would they say if they were narrating your life right now?

Let them speak louder.

## Step 3: Turn the Dials

Now we do the recalibration, as if you are at the mixing board in a sound studio. Draw two columns. In one, list the voices you want to *turn down*. In the other, the ones you want to *turn up*.

This doesn't mean you cut people out of your life (though sometimes you will). It means you change the *weight* their voice has in your internal world.

You're in charge of the volume now.

Use the following prompts to turn the dial intentionally.

To Turn Down a Voice:

- "This voice is based on fear, not truth."
- "I understand where it came from, but I don't have to carry it anymore."

- "They were wrong about me."
- "I choose growth over safety."

**To Turn Up a Voice:**

- "This voice reminds me of who I *really* am."
- "Their belief in me is rooted in love and clarity."
- "This voice feels like home—expansive, not shrinking."
- "I want to sound more like *this* when I speak to myself."

## Step 4: Build Your Inner Soundtrack

Here's where the real shift happens.

Start creating a new *internal playlist*—a mental track list of encouragement, clarity, and power to get stuck in your head. These phrases and beliefs speak directly to the life you're building. They should be the background noise.

Write the "tracks" for your new inner voice. They could sound like:

- "I am allowed to take up space."
- "I don't need anyone else's permission to go after what I want."
- "What I imagine is valid—and I'm capable of creating it."
- "Their limitations are not my truth."
- "I trust myself to figure it out."

Repeat them. Make them louder. Say them out loud if you need to. Use them like armor when the old voices creep back in. And they will. But now you're equipped.

Now you know how to change the station.

This isn't a one-time exercise. It's a ritual. The more you tune in, the more you notice who you're letting speak on your behalf, and whether they deserve to be there.

Because your life becomes what you listen to. And you deserve a life that sounds like *truth*, *beauty*, and *power*. Not fear. So, be bold enough to ask: Whose voice is narrating my story? And is it time for a new narrator?

# 23.

# Surround Yourself with Quality People

*It's Your World, You Decide Who Lives in It*

There's a saying: you are the company you keep. I never gave it much thought when I was younger. I assumed my friends didn't have to affect me because I could still be my own person, separate from the people I surrounded myself with. But the truth is, no one is immune. Not really. And the people in our lives shape us more than we realize.

They can lift us, or they can pull us under. And when you've spent years around toxic people, you don't just leave with a few bruises—you go with scars that can dramatically shape how you see yourself and the world around you.

I've had my share of toxic relationships—friends who disguised their jealousy as concern, partners who made me question my worth, and people who claimed to love me while making me feel like shit. People who I had to shrink myself around to fit their version of who I should be. The scariest part? I didn't always see it.

That's the thing about toxicity—it's not always obvious. It seeps into your life slowly, like a leak in the ceiling you don't notice until the whole house starts to collapse.

When you're around people who belittle you, doubt you, or make you feel like you're never enough, you start to believe them. Their words become your inner voice. You hesitate before speaking because you expect to be dismissed. You second-guess your dreams because they've convinced you they're too big. You start apologizing for who you are, not even realizing you're doing it.

And for me, it always showed in the way I looked.

I can look back at photos of myself and immediately know what kind of relationship I was in at the time. It's written all over my face. The times I was with someone who drained me and made me feel small, I can see it in my eyes—dull, lifeless, tired. My smile didn't quite reach. My posture was different, like I was subconsciously making myself smaller. Even my style would change, almost as if I were trying to disappear. I would stop putting effort into myself, or worse, I'd try too hard, using my appearance as a mask. Hoping that if I looked together enough, no one would notice how much I was falling apart.

But when I was around the right people, the difference was undeniable. My eyes lit up. My body language was open and free. My confidence radiated. How we feel inside always finds a way to show on the outside, whether we realize it or not.

It took time to unlearn the social patterns I had fallen into. I had to recognize that I was attracting the wrong relationships because, deep down, I didn't believe I deserved better. I had to stop seeking approval from those who would never give it. I had to stop picking broken people to fix us both. I had to start finding my worth in myself.

And when I did that—when I started setting boundaries, walking away from toxic relationships, and surrounding myself with people who truly saw me—I felt the difference. There was a lightness and peace that I hadn't felt before. I started sensing toxicity before I was enmeshed in it. I became discerning about which people to share my peace with.

I became protective of myself the way I had always protected others.

I spoke earlier in the book about being in alignment to attract the things you want. Well, once I was finally in alignment with myself, the people who started appearing in my life matched my level. They were kind, authentic, and loyal while still being ambitious. They were adventurous, engaging, and driven without being opportunistic.

The right people won't make you question your worth; they will remind you of it. They don't want to compete with your shine—they want to amplify it. They will challenge you in ways that feel expansive, not diminishing. They carry peace, not projection.

That kind of energy is transformative. It's stabilizing. It's rare—but it's real.

Now, if you're reading this and thinking, *I don't have people like that*, I hear you. I know what it's like to walk into a room and feel like no one sees you. To believe your uniqueness makes you incompatible with connection. To convince yourself you're better off alone, even when solitude starts to wear thin.

But I promise you this: you're not so rare that no one will ever understand you. You just haven't found your people yet.

And here's the truth no one tells you:

*You can't find your people if you're
too busy playing a version of yourself
built for survival, not connection.*

You have to let the real version of you step forward. You have to go where your energy feels natural, not managed. You have to be visible, even when it's vulnerable. Because your people? They're out there. But they're not going to find you behind someone else's expectations.

You need to go to the places where you shine and let that light hit you.

When you find your people, all the loneliness and heartache from isolation will disappear as if it were never there. And believe me, waiting for the right people is better than settling for the wrong ones. The placeholders and wrong people are just put in your path, so you have context for when you stumble upon the greats.

It's like finding your signature scent, the best pair of jeans, or the perfect white T-shirt. It's like finally discovering the perfect tailoring after years of off-the-rack compromises. It's the feeling of alignment, aesthetically and emotionally. Everything fits.

The right people will not require you to dull your shine to keep the peace. They *are* the peace.

The most gratifying rewards of life come after the long road you've walked to reach them.

If I could tell my younger self one thing, it would be this: You don't owe anyone access to your light. You don't have to prove your worth to people who can't recognize it. And the quality of your life will rise or fall depending on who's sitting next to you.

Choose wisely. Choose intentionally.

Because the company you keep becomes the tone, the texture, the temperature of your life.

And if your reflection has felt off lately, it might not be you. It might be the room.

People don't just touch your life—they imprint it. Quietly, persistently. In the smallest habits, the subtlest beliefs, the way you see yourself in the mirror when no one else is watching.

And no one leaves a more profound imprint than the person you choose to build your life beside. That's why choosing the right life partner is everything.

We talk about love, chemistry, compatibility, and shared values, but beyond the poetry and the performance, your life partner is the one who you give a blueprint of your life. They influence the architecture of your confidence. They shape the cadence of your days. And over time, if you're not careful, they can either elevate your energy or drain it so subtly that you forget what light feels like.

I've seen it up close in my clients—how a relationship can alter the way someone moves through the world. That's what the right partner does.

When you find not just someone who saves you, but someone who *sees* and encourages you. Someone who doesn't just allow you to grow, but expects it. Maybe the relationship has its bumps in the road (as does everyone's). But it's clear that they loved it when you take up space, dress loud, and disagree with you. In this person's presence, you don't have to overcompensate or shrink. You just . . . exist. Fully. Boldly. Softly. Or however you choose to exist, without consequence.

They don't define your identity, but they *hold space* for it. They don't hold a fixed point for your confidence, but *make room* for it to grow.

The wrong person will have you doubting your instincts, shrinking your dreams, and editing your personality to maintain the peace. You'll start questioning if your ambition is too much. If your needs are unreasonable. If maybe, just maybe, the dullness you feel is your fault.

But the right person? They'll have you returning to yourself.

And that return—that realignment—isn't dramatic. It's elegant. Almost unnoticeable at first. You start sleeping better. Your laugh comes back. You start dressing for yourself again. You experiment. You speak without second-guessing—your posture changes. Your eyes shift. Everything recalibrates.

It's like your life is finally tailored properly.

And don't get me wrong—it's not about fairy tales. This isn't about perfect relationships or the absence of conflict. It's about emotional safety. Emotional *style*, if you will. The kind of relationship that's built on clarity, not chaos. Substance over spectacle.

And if you're currently in something that feels off—where you're always walking carefully on eggshells, holding your breath, trying to fit a mold that was never made for you— know this:

You deserve a partner who reflects you to yourself with clarity, not distortion. Someone who holds up a mirror that says, *This is who you are—and you are enough.* Someone who doesn't need to be the star because they understand you both shine brighter together.

That's the love that changes your outlook. Your energy. That's the love that feels like coming home to yourself. And if you're still waiting for that person, wait well. Don't settle for the placeholder. Don't dull your edge. Don't tuck away the parts of yourself that feel inconvenient. The right one will love the whole masterpiece, not the watered-down or filtered version, but *the entire expression.*

And when you find them, you'll know.

Not because your world suddenly becomes perfect, but because you will. Not perfect as in flawless. Perfect as in whole. Integrated. Alive.

Like the best cut, color, and styling, it doesn't transform you into someone new. It reveals who you were all along.

## 24.

# Master Your Mindset and the Art of Being You

*You Are a Masterpiece Waiting to Be Unveiled*

P eople always ask me: *How do you do it?* How can you step into a room with some of the most famous people in the world, hold their public image in your hands, and not crack under pressure?

The truth is, I don't just walk in and hope for the best. I get into a headspace where failure isn't an option.

When I step into a high-stakes situation—whether it's a *Vogue* cover, the Met Gala, or working with a new uber-famous client— I don't allow doubt to enter the room with me. Nerves are natural, but I don't let them control me. Instead, I turn them into fuel. I remind myself: You're here for a reason. They trust you. You know what you're doing. That mindset is everything.

To get into the right headspace for my work takes preparation. Because of my anxiety, I like to have as much information as I can about what I'm going into so I can be more present.

I never show up without a vision. Before meeting clients, I study their faces, styles, past looks, and current moods. I think about what they want to say with their hair. What identity or story are they trying to tell for this specific event or occasion?

I also visualize. I picture the entire process before I even pick up a brush. I see my hands moving with precision, the hair transforming, the moment they look in the mirror and light up. That mental rehearsal is everything for me.

And then, when the time comes, I take a deep breath and commit. My movements have no hesitation because hesitation is the fastest way to lose trust. If you move with confidence, people feel safe with you.

One of the biggest lessons I've learned is this:

### *Your energy is contagious.*

The client feels it if I walk into a room unsure of myself. But they relax if I walk in grounded, focused, and excited.

Much of my success comes from the safety my clients feel when they are in my hands. They know I've got them, and I know how to make them look beautiful. They trust me.

Walking into a room with a new A-list client can feel like stepping onto a stage with the whole world watching. But having courage isn't about being fearless; it's about knowing your worth despite the fear. That goes for any setting: romantic, professional, or interpersonal.

When I first moved to Los Angeles, I got a call to do Christina Aguilera's hair for *The Voice*. I had done celebrities before, but this was on a new level of stardom. Not only was Christina an icon, but *The Voice* was one of the biggest television shows, so millions of people would see her hair.

When I arrived at *The Voice*, three hours were allocated in the schedule for glam. The makeup artist entered Christina's trailer first, and I was left outside, waiting. The first hour passed, and I told myself that was to be expected. I was sure I would be called in soon. Then another hour went by, and I was feeling quite anxious by that time. I had never met Christina Aguilera and I wanted to do a great job, so hopefully, I'd be asked back.

As the clock continued to tick, my nerves frayed. I had prepared for the job—was I ever going to be allowed in the room to actually do it?

Another half hour passed.

Twenty minutes before the live show began, Christina called me in the trailer to do her hair. I imagined that her hair must already be done or would be looking good already. I probably just needed to brush it into place, add a few well-placed curls, and give it a "last look" once-over. Because what else was there to do in no time?

That was not the case at all.

Her hair hadn't been touched. It needed something major to match the glam of her makeup and outfit. Fear took over my body. I did that thing that hairdressers do when they start just moving the hair around, hoping something's gonna happen. There was no way I could execute something worthy of her status in time.

Thankfully, I'd spent the whole day before prepping different wigs and hairpieces, in case Christina wanted to try something different, or if her hair was damaged.

I asked Christina, "Have you ever tried a wig?"

"Yeah, I don't like wigs," Christina said as she waited for me to do something.

Internally, I started spinning. Of course Christina Aguilera doesn't like wigs. *In fact, why would you like anything I do? I'm just a boy from Leicester, England. What was I doing here?*

Then I remembered a conversation I had earlier that day with Kate, the mother of my kids. She said, "Remember when you were younger, questioning if you belonged in those rooms with people like Christina Aguilera? You're there now. Show her what you can do. Otherwise you'll have to come back home."

She was right. It was my job to make Christina Aguilera look her best. I would kick myself for eternity if I hadn't pushed for the wig and let her go out with half-done hair. I hadn't come this far only to come this far. If I didn't make this work, I would need to return to England because I was running out of money.

I took a breath and summoned my confidence, mentally drawing on everything I knew about my strengths and my instincts. Then, I turned to Christina and said, "You've never tried one of my wigs."

I pulled out a long platinum ash blonde wig with a side part and a soft curl at the ends. It looked glamorous, sophisticated, and edgy, just like Christina.

She was intrigued, and her stylist looked over and said she thought it was cool. I pinned the wig on Christina's head with ten minutes left before the live show started. She looked beautiful, and the wig looked natural on her head and perfect with her style. My only concern now was whether Christina was happy and comfortable in the wig. Unfortunately, it all happened so fast that I had no idea how Christina felt before she was rushed onstage. I prayed the wig would stay on her head. I had no idea if she was sitting in her judge's chair or would be performing and possibly shake it off by accident.

I held my breath waiting for the show to end, scrutinizing Christina from the monitors for any sign the wig was loose, and thankfully it never budged.

After the show, I saw Christina standing down the hallway. She looked back at me. My heart pounded.

"Everyone likes your wig," she said, giving me that iconic smirk of hers.

My insides nearly burst with the rush of relief and pride. It was truly a pivotal moment in my career. I had prepared for this job, for this giant opportunity, and when faced with challenges, fear, and self-doubt, I relied on my training and talent. I was an educated professional with a point of view, not the boy from Leicester afraid to make a fuss or ruffle a feather.

That was a turning point for me. That was the job that cemented my confidence in myself. But take note: my confidence didn't come as a result of the *outcome* of that situation. In the actual moment, I couldn't afford to wait and find out if I'd succeed or not. I had to channel that confidence right then, *before* I even tried the wig on her.

A self-secure and effective mindset can't be earned by success— you need to put yourself in that mindset on the front end.

That job changed my life. If I hadn't risen to the moment, I probably would have gone back to England and not had the life or career that I have now.

Mastering the art of being yourself will be a unique process. Nurturing your strengths and finding all the ways you shine is an ongoing practice, not unlike meditation. I genuinely believe, because this has been my experience, that confidence and success will follow when you do the work and show up prepared.

After that job, Christina Aguilera booked me again and again.


I get that there's something addictive about looking at others, especially when it feels like they've got it all figured out. You see them thriving in their careers, posting about their perfect relationships, or flexing their latest accomplishments, and suddenly, you're spiraling.

But here's another pro tip:

*You can't run your race if you're too busy watching someone else run theirs.*

But their journey isn't your journey. Your life, goals, purpose, and path are uniquely yours, and when you get caught up in comparing yourself to others, you lose focus. You dilute your power. Most importantly, you block yourself from the one thing that will bring you the peace and progress you want, which is alignment with yourself.

When you're too busy watching other people, you stop listening to the quiet voice inside you—the one guiding you toward your goals, growth, and best life. This is the voice you need to be attuned to. Not the one that tells you that someone's LinkedIn postings are your benchmarks, or their Instagram highlight reel is your reality check.

I know it's hard to ignore the noise. Social media, family expectations, the pressure of living up to someone else's idea of success—it's all around us. But let's be real for a second: None of that is your business.

The key to actual progress—whether it's internal growth, achieving your professional goals, or building meaningful relationships—is to keep your eyes on your own paper. Focus on your lane. If you're constantly glancing to the side to see what others are doing, you'll either trip, fall behind, or take the wrong turn. And all of that adds up to *stress*, *anxiety*, and *exhaustion*.

## HOW TO MASTER YOUR MINDSET
### Step One: Recognize Your Triggers

We all have specific triggers that send us into comparison mode. Maybe it's a social media post about a party from someone who seems like they have a way bigger circle of friends than you. Perhaps it's a friend who always seems ahead in their job, getting promotions and hitting milestones you feel you are nowhere near.

Take a moment and reflect: When are you the most tempted to compare yourself to others?

- Is it when you're feeling insecure about your appearance or social status?
- Is it when you're doubting your ability to succeed?
- Is it when you're not seeing immediate results, and someone else's success stings too much?

Write down the moments that lead you to look outward, and pay attention to how you feel afterward. Do you feel deflated, frustrated, inadequate? Becoming aware of these feelings and their roots is the first step to dismantling them.

Here's the truth: When we look outward, we neglect the only thing we can truly control: ourselves.

## Step Two: Take Back Your Energy

Every time you look at someone else's progress, success, or story, picture yourself literally giving them some of your tangible store of energy. It's easy to tell ourselves that their success inspires us, but deep down, it often comes with envy, resentment, or self-doubt. And that's draining. That's energy you could be using to fuel your vision and actually get closer to achieving it.

If you're giving away your energy to someone else's journey, you'll find yourself running on empty when it comes to your own. So, here are some practical ways you can reclaim that energy:

1. **Stop scrolling.** I know, you hear it everywhere, but it's for a reason! If scrolling through social media leaves you feeling less than, cut back. We're not meant to be exposed to so many people's personal

lives and accomplishments. It's exposure overload.
It's okay to unfollow or mute accounts that make
you feel less than stellar about your progress. It doesn't
make you weak.

2. **Limit your exposure to external pressures.** This might
   mean setting boundaries with people, whether it's
   family members, friends, or coworkers, who make
   you feel like you're not doing enough, or not doing
   it fast enough. You get to choose who you allow
   into your energy field.

3. **Refocus your gaze.** Shift your attention back to
   yourself. Instead of spending energy *looking outward*,
   start focusing inward. What do you want? What's
   the next best step for you? What's the prize in front
   of you that's actually deserving of your gaze?

## Step Three: Redefine Your Success

If you're constantly measuring yourself against someone else's
version of success, you'll never honestly know what success *feels*
like. You'll always be in someone else's shadow.

So what does it look like to start defining success on your
terms?

Success isn't about hitting milestones just because everyone
else is. It's about moving toward a life that feels authentic, meaningful, and aligned with who you are. It's about building something that lights you up inside—something that excites you and
feels *right*.

It might not match anyone else's. And that's precisely how it
should be. You have permission to carve out your path.

When you're clear on your goals and priorities, the opinions
of others won't have the power to shake you. You'll know ex-

actly what you're working toward—and that's where the peace comes in.

### Step Four: Celebrate Your Progress, Big or Small

Another key to keeping your eyes on your paper is celebrating your progress. I'm talking about every little win, no matter how small it seems. Did you get through a tough day with a smile on your face? Celebrate it. Did you update something on your résumé? Celebrate it. Did you make a decision that aligned with your values? Celebrate it.

The more you focus on your growth and steps forward, the less you'll feel the need to compare. Success is a journey, not a destination, and when you start appreciating the *small victories* along the way, you create a momentum that feels good—no comparison needed.

### Step Five: Build Your Inner Circle (aka the People You Keep) Carefully

If you're consistently focused on your progress, the next natural step is building relationships that can align with your vision and even support it. You need to surround yourself with people who encourage your growth, not ones who constantly distract you from it. Relationships that cohere with your goals and your values can help you stay on track and motivate you to keep going.

Even if your friends don't have the exact same goals as you, the key here is that they should be people who are genuinely rooting for your success, not ones who are competing with you, or worse, trying to pull you back to a version of yourself you're trying to leave behind.

Ask yourself:

- Who in my life lifts me?
- Who do I feel like my authentic self around?
- Who celebrates my wins and cheers me on?
- Who challenges me to grow in healthy ways?
- Who supports my dreams, not just with words but with actions?

Build your inner circle with those people. And remember, this circle doesn't have to be big. It just needs to be real and supportive.

You reclaim your peace when you stop comparing your life to someone else's. You stop measuring your worth against theirs. You stop letting *their* journey dictate your feelings of adequacy.

Your journey, goals, and path are uniquely yours, and they deserve your full attention.

Ultimately, the only race you're running is where you cross the finish line of your potential. And trust me, *that* is the most fulfilling victory you'll ever experience.

# 25.

# When We Polish, We Shine

## *Reclaiming the Gleam You've Always Had*

She wasn't one for overstatement. She had never been the kind of person to make grand gestures or speak in sweeping declarations. She'd always had this quiet, deliberate energy about her. She had a sense of calm control that drew people in without demanding attention.

You could tell she didn't really *care* about her hair. She wore it like an afterthought. She'd come in, time and time again, asking for the same cut, the same treatment. A trim here, a little color there. She took the same approach to many things: good enough—*fine*—but never polished.

One day, I asked her if I could do something different.

"Do whatever you want. I don't care." She barely looked up from her phone.

So, I did. I lifted the weight off her hair, reshaped it, and brought in some subtle layers to give it light, life. I added a bit of warmth to her color, just enough to catch the light, like a slight shift that made everything feel *intentional*. The change wasn't huge, but it was enough. A little polish. A little effort. It wasn't about transforming her, but giving what was already there a chance to shine.

She sized up her new hair when I was finished. "Wow. Why didn't you do this last time or the five times before that?"

"Because," I laughed, "you never let me do anything besides the usual before."

A few weeks later, I bumped into her at a coffee shop. It was like running into someone who'd suddenly leveled up. She was glowing, not just from the outside, though that was undeniable. Her whole vibe was visibly different.

"You look amazing," I said, unable to hide my surprise. "What's going on?"

She paused, a slow smile spreading across her face. "It's funny, I've been thinking a lot about that haircut you gave me. At first, I thought it was just hair, that I looked more put together. But then I noticed how everything I did felt more . . . pointed. Like I was trying to match my haircut. Does that make sense?"

"It makes complete sense. You were being intentional because your hair reads like a choice, not an afterthought."

"What you did to my hair kind of woke something in me." She laughed, shaking her head like she couldn't quite believe it. "I started looking at other parts of my life and realized I needed to up my game. Even the little things, like I just redid my book-shelves, so they can look more like something from a design magazine. I did horizontal stacks of books, little cool trinkets, photos. It's dumb, but it makes me feel cool."

I told her I totally get it. Polishing the things in your life can spark a domino effect. It doesn't have to be about reinventing everything; it can just be about refining and paying attention to the details that make a difference—and then you'll get inspired to keep doing it in other areas.

She had always had potential, but she'd been holding back with-out realizing it. It wasn't until she started with something as simple as her hair—giving it attention and intention—that she began to unlock the next level of herself. She told me that more than just the bookshelves, she was making her home feel more curated. She was pushing herself more at work and feeling invigorated.

Small, deliberate actions can transform everything around you. It can ignite a ripple effect and spark a new way of thinking.

The more attention we give to the details, the clearer the some-times nonexistent or obtuse path becomes. The act of polishing forces you to pay attention, to slow down, and get intentional. It reminds you that nothing is static; everything has the potential to be more, to be better, to be *you*, but with a little extra care.

## POLISH ONE THING

I tell everyone that if you don't like what you see in the mirror, polish one thing. That's what I do when I'm not feeling it for myself. Moisturize your skin, brush your hair, put on your fa-vorite sweater, pick anything! *Polish one thing.* When you polish something, it may not get radically transformed into something else—but maybe it doesn't *need* to be something else. Maybe you just need to create the opportunity for it to shine. And shin-ing not only attracts but, more importantly, it feels damn good.

*Remember: No one is holding you hostage
to the qualities you dislike but you.*

Polishing is like cleaning the smudge off a window so you can see clearly. Or think of it like this: You have a piece of wood that's weathered, scratched, and worn. It's not perfect, but the unique beauty is still there; you just have to put in work to bring it out. You sand it, clean it up, and with some care, it starts glow-ing with life. The wood didn't change; what changed is how you see it and how it feels.

To polish isn't to change the essence; it's to reveal its hidden potential.

That's what polishing is like in life—it's not about overhauling everything. It's tending to the details, making minor adjustments, and amplifying the qualities that already exist within you. It's taking the good stuff you already have, cleaning it up, and making it work better.

Like so much else, your hair is a perfect metaphor for this idea. I'm sure you've noticed that when you take the time to care for it, whether it's through blow-drying it after a shower, regular trims, nourishing treatments, or styling it every now and then—it feels different. It gives you a sense of control, it gives you confidence. That confidence affects how others perceive you and how you engage with the world. It's not just how it looks: a well-groomed hairstyle can change your entire presence.

But polishing isn't just for hair; it's a philosophy that can be applied to everything in life—and one that synthesizes so many ideas we've talked about already in this book.

Consider, for example, how the act of polishing requires *intention*. A messy bun, the "I don't care" look, can be just as polished in its own right if it's purposeful. If it reflects the attitude you want to convey, then it's polished. It's the opposite of laziness or negligence. It's a conscious choice.

As a result of that intentionality, when you're getting ready for something important—a meeting, a date, or a moment when you want to show up as your most empowered self—polishing becomes a tool of transformation. A new manicure or fresh hairstyle doesn't just elevate your appearance; it boosts your self-esteem because you feel more put together and in control. You're setting a clear intention for how you present yourself.

Polishing also isn't about trying to achieve perfection—it's about progress, like we talked about in chapter thirteen. Polishing, in its truest sense, is about *refinement*. It's about taking what is already there and elevating it. It's about putting in the work to bring out the best version of something.

It also brings in the idea of *alignment*. You're not just polishing those small details. You're aligning with your purpose. How you show up externally reflects how you feel internally. When you polish the outside—your hair, clothes, skin—your inside often follows suit.

## WHAT LOOKS UNPOLISHED?

So look in the mirror. Examine the current makeup of your days, your relationships, your style. Nearly everything about us can benefit from a shine and touch-up somewhere. Make a list of what you're unhappy with and just polish one thing:

Dislike the color of your eyes? Get colored contacts, or shop for a pair of colorful glasses to bring your eyes a new frame.

Feel uncomfortable in your body? Do things that are good for you. Drink more water, eat cleaner, get more sleep. Give your body a chance to feel good. If you want to change or tone your body, start with something manageable like doing ten push-ups and sit-ups before bed—or if you don't, then invest in different kinds of clothing that flatter and make you feel powerful, or some shapewear that enhances your best assets.

Hate that you get quiet at social gatherings and parties? Think of a few engaging conversation starters that you feel knowledgeable about.

Hate that you're scatterbrained and things keep falling through the cracks? Set aside one hour every Sunday to get organized for the week.

Beyond small, daily actions like these, the act of polishing can be applied to bigger areas of life as well:

### What You Do

Let's move beyond your hair and talk about your career. Imagine you've been doing the same thing for years, coasting through your job as a financial analyst or your catering business without much excitement or growth. You've got skills and competence, but maybe you feel trapped in the same stagnant routine. The passion fizzled out, you've stopped growing and learning. So what does it look like to invest in yourself again and start polishing things?

It could mean learning a new skill to get a side hustle, attending or speaking at workshops, networking with other companies, updating your résumé, or even just tweaking your daily routine so that you're more efficient. Maybe it's adopting better work-life balance, reducing procrastination, or setting more intentional deadlines for your goals.

When you polish your approach, you tell the universe, "I'm here to make an impact." You're investing in yourself, and the momentum you build begins to ripple out into your work and interactions. It's not about waiting for a promotion or external validation; it's about not being complacent and bringing your A-game again.

You'll notice that your energy shifts from passive to active. And believe me, that shift in mindset is noticeable. People see it. You start looking for opportunities you weren't noticing before.

Eventually, your career isn't just a job anymore; it becomes a platform where you can grow and make an impact.

## Where You Are

Now, take that concept and apply it to your home. Life can get chaotic. Clutter piles up on the kitchen counter. Laundry accumulates daily. Dust gathers in places we don't notice anymore. It's easy to ignore, especially when the demands of life feel overwhelming. But have you ever noticed how much better you feel when you take the time to tidy up or organize? How clear your mind becomes and how your nervous system calms?

If you constantly live in disarray, it's your life looking back at you reflecting your inner world. But when you take the time to polish your environment, you create a sanctuary where you can relax, recharge, and focus. Take care of the space you live in and polish your home, because you're really taking care of yourself.

Whether it's dusting off that one piece of furniture that's been neglected for months or cleaning up some clutter while you watch Netflix reruns, you'll find the space doesn't just look better, it feels better. It doesn't mean adding new things or buying fancy decor. It's about taking care of what you already have. A clean, organized space fosters clarity for the life you're cultivating.

## How You Feel

Here's another big one: your mental and emotional state. Just as your physical space can become cluttered and chaotic, so can your mind. Over time, negative thoughts, self-doubt, old stories, and damaging beliefs can cloud your judgment and sense of self. So how can you polish your thoughts and emotions to bring out your true self?

Maybe this means challenging the negativity that holds you back, the self-criticism that undermines your confidence, and the limiting beliefs that create barriers between you and your potential.

The same way you wouldn't let dust and fingerprints accumulate on a mirror, making it impossible to see yourself, you shouldn't let negative self-talk build up in your mind. Instead, actively practice positive self-talk. Challenge old stories that no longer align with who you are today and replace them with healthier, more empowering ones like we've talked about. Give yourself the same care and attention you give your hair, home, and career.

When you take the time to work on your mindset, you polish the way you see yourself, too. You have more clarity, a new light.

At its core, polishing is about small, daily actions. It's showing up for yourself consistently and putting in the effort to refine the parts of you that matter. Polishing is about progress and growth. It's taking what you already have—the talents, the relationships, the resources—and refining them to help you gleam.

When you do that, the results are undeniable. You see your worth, your goals, and your purpose more clearly. You show up more confidently in every area of your life.

# 26.

# When the Path Doesn't Appear, Build Your Own Bridge

*Cross Over to the Life That's Waiting for You*

As a kid, you naturally believe the world is a playground full of possibilities. You don't know the meaning of limits. You're born with this invisible, infinite horizon stretching out before you—a place where anything can happen. There's no divide between what you imagine and what you believe you can achieve.

You dream big, with the pure energy of innocence, without the burdens of doubt, judgment, or fear. You're an astronaut on Mars, a superhero saving the world, an adventurer exploring the jungle, a pop star on stage. It all feels real, attainable.

Failure is not even a thought. It doesn't exist in your vocabulary. Life hasn't knocked you around yet. You haven't felt the sting of rejection, the crushing weight of disappointment, the hurt of betrayal, or the suffocating pressure of expectation. Everything is within reach if you stretch far enough.

Then, life starts to happen.

You grow up and see that things aren't as simple as they once seemed. The messages you get about what's "practical" and what's "actually possible" become the prominent ones. Reality, with its infinite shades of gray, pokes holes in your once unshakable optimism. The wide-eyed dreams start to seem naive and unrealistic—and slowly fade into skepticism.

You no longer stretch yourself beyond what's comfortable. Instead, you start believing you can only be something that fits into the little boxes life hands you. You get a job, have bills, and responsibilities that come with their own set of expectations.

It's a slow fade.

The dreams you had for yourself—those visions of who you could be, the life you *wanted* to live—get pushed aside. The untainted aspirations of your childhood give way to the logistics of survival. Ambition takes a back seat to practicality.

You act with caution. You lose your spark. That wild, untamed fire inside you gets buried beneath all the noise of being responsible. That voice inside you that once roared becomes the quiet voice of reason, saying, *Maybe this is good enough.* But is it?

## SPECTATOR OR PLAYER?

Maybe instead of settling, you're stuck in a state of fear. I've seen it happen to so many people, myself included. You get stuck in a state of perpetual dreaming—constantly thinking about the life you want but can't seem to get around to actually living.

Before you know it, you've become a spectator. You're watching others chase their dreams, take risks, fall, get back up, and make something of their lives while you stay in the safety of the sidelines.

At first, the spectator role is comfortable. The seat's nice, and the view is excellent. You don't have to put yourself out there, you're not vulnerable to rejection, failure, or disappointment. You can avoid heartbreak. It's safe. But eventually, the view from the stands isn't enough, and the comfort fades.

What then?

The spectator gets to live in the world of *what could have been*—always wondering, always wishing, but never living. And let me tell you, watching others chase their dreams feels hollow. You want to be in the game. You want to be playing.

From my experience, lack of action is rarely about a lack of ability and is more about fear. It's the fear that you aren't *worthy* of the successes you dream of. It's the fear that you don't have what it takes or that your dreams are too big for someone like you. It's the fear that you aren't enough, that the obstacles are too significant, and that the path ahead is too unclear. I have more to say about "the path"; just wait.

In truth, obstacles exist whether you try or not. Whether you stay a spectator in the stands or step onto the field of dreams, people will still throw challenges at you. Life is unpredictable, unfair, messy, and annoyingly relentless. You'll get knocked down. You'll fail.

The difference is, when you're in the game, you get to choose how to approach those challenges and obstacles. When you fail on the field, you will also grow better as a result. When you get knocked down, you will rise stronger. That's how it works—you're doing things, taking risks, facing your challenges head-on, and the growth is so much better because of it.

You only get one shot at this life. If you're reading this and wondering whether it's too late to start or too late to chase your dreams—or if you're waiting for the "right moment"—let me set you straight: there's no such thing as the right moment. There is only now. If you wait until everything is just right, you'll be waiting forever.

Your dreams don't fulfill themselves. You need to get in the arena. You need to stop watching and start doing. You will never taste the rewards of overcoming the hard things if you stay in the prison of the sidelines.

But how?

## BE YOUR OWN ARCHITECT

Everyone loves to talk about finding your "path," like it's some obvious thing you stumble upon. Just a neat little road that leads you straight to the life you want. *Find your path. Stay on your path. Don't lose your path.*

But what if there is no path?

What if you wake up one day and realize there's no clear-cut trail that was always meant for you? No map. No blueprint. No neon arrow pointing you toward the life you want. Just a vast space up ahead, a wide stretch of foggy nothingness, with only a quiet voice inside you saying, *This isn't it. But I don't know where it is, either.*

No one talks about this part, where you must build your bridge. And it sucks.

Plank by plank. Messy and makeshift at first. With splinters in your hands and wind in your face. No guarantee that it's going to work. No clear destination. Just faith, sweat, and the audacity to believe there's something better waiting for you on the other side.

That's the kind of life I know intimately. The one you build from scratch. The kind where nothing feels handed to you. Where the path forward isn't visible, but the pull forward is undeniable. One nail, one step, one decision at a time—and yes, it's been full of failure along the way, but far more rewarding.

There's something terrifying about not seeing where you're going. When I think of my journey, I see myself standing on the edge of what was—my life as a straight man, fearing my truth, standing in a salon filled with these big dreams of being a respected top stylist, staring into the blank space of what could be. The future I dreamed of hadn't fully arrived yet. I knew I couldn't stay there, but moving forward felt like stepping into midair.

*That space? That's where
the bridge begins.*

You don't need a master plan. You need a start. You need one plank. One bold step or decision that says, *I'm not staying here anymore.* Maybe it's applying to a job you don't feel "ready" for. Perhaps it's finally moving to that city that's been calling you for years. Maybe it's ending the relationship you've outgrown even though the unknowns ahead are scary, or investing in the version of yourself you've kept on the back burner.

Whatever it is, that first plank is the hardest to lay. But once it's down? The rest follows.

Momentum is a builder's best friend.

I had a client who came to me during what she called her "gray period." That's how she described it. Her hair was faded, her skin dull, her wardrobe muted to the point of invisibility. She'd just turned thirty-eight and was recently divorced. Two kids. A steady but uninspiring job in finance.

She said she felt like she was "living someone else's life." Not in a dramatic way. Just in that quiet, soul-level exhaustion kind of way. She had everything she thought she was supposed to want. But none of it felt like *her.*

When I asked her what she *really* wanted, she whispered it like it was dangerous.

"I want to be a chef. A real one. I want to move to Lisbon and open a tiny, beautiful restaurant." She laughed immediately after, brushing it off. "Ridiculous, I know."

But it wasn't ridiculous. It was hers. It was real. And it was possible.

There was no bridge to that life, though, I told my client. Not from where she stood. She didn't have a culinary degree. She didn't speak Portuguese. She didn't have a trust fund waiting to catch her. But she had something more important: she had a spark. And that was enough to start.

Over the next year, she worked on her dream—building her bridge slowly, steadily, one plank at a time. She cooked for fun on weekends and evenings after the kids went to bed. She posted recipes online. She enrolled in a part-time culinary program. She joined online groups of expats living in Portugal. She started downsizing her house, saving every extra penny she could.

It wasn't easy. It wasn't glamorous. It didn't go viral.

But plank by plank, the bridge started to form.

Two years later, she packed up their life and moved to Lisbon. She opened a tiny kitchen that seats fourteen. It's simple. It's beautiful. And it's filled with the joy of someone who believed in her dreams enough to build the damn bridge.

She sends me pictures sometimes. Her hair is pulled back, her face flushed from the heat of the kitchen, and she is grinning from behind a pot of something gorgeous and simmering. She reminds me of the power of small actions, one day at a time—the power of deciding *I am worthy of this life.* And if you keep going, the bridge stops being temporary and becomes life itself—not the detour, not the fantasy, the *reality.*


Most people don't build bridges; they stand on the edge of their discomfort and stay there, hoping someone else will rescue them.

But you're not most people. If you were, you wouldn't care so much about bettering yourself. You probably wouldn't be reading this book.

You don't need to see the whole path. You don't need to have it all figured out. You just need to start. One step. One plank. One small act of courage that says, *I am worthy of something more.*

When you do, something will shift inside you. You start trusting yourself more. You begin seeing doors where there used to be walls. You stop waiting for permission. You become the architect of your own life.

Not a spectator. Not a drifter. A builder. Someone who doesn't just imagine the life they want—they construct it. If the path isn't clear, and the road isn't visible, don't wait.

You don't need a blueprint. You need a beginning.

You need one action that says: I'm not staying here.

So, if you're standing on the edge, staring into the fog, and not sure where to start, this exercise is for you.

---

### HOW YOU BUILD YOUR BRIDGE

1. **Name It.**
   Get bold. What's the dream? The real one, not the edited version. Write it down. Make it vivid. How does it taste? What does it feel like when you get it? Smell it. Hear it. Live in it.

2. **Release Your Fear Inventory.**
   List every fear, every worry, every "what if." Then dig deep—where did that fear come from? Is it real? Is it true? What evidence do you have that says it isn't?

3. **Break Down the Obstacles.**
   Don't let the boulder scare you. Break it into pebbles. What are the smaller pieces? What are the baby steps?

4. **Count Your Tools.**
   What skills do you already have? Who's in your corner? What do you need to learn? Get strategic— but don't get stuck here. You're not writing a thesis, you're writing your life.

5. **Control the Controllables.**
   Spoiler: You can't control outcomes. You can control your actions, your effort, and your attitude. So do that.

6. **Take Action.**
   Make a move. Today. Track your progress, even if it's messy. Especially if it's messy.

Many people go through their daily lives unconsciously or without knowing who they are. They're living the life they were taught and programmed to have as a child. They're tied down by their roots, their mistakes, their pasts. You don't have to be one of them.

*Your messes are where*
*the real story lives.*

When you realize those ideas, those roots, don't have to define you, and you can evolve in your physical, mental, and emotional form, the result is life-changing.

In my experience, once someone feels seen, they want to make more changes. This book is my way of saying, I see you.

Now get busy! You have a bridge to build.

# Epilogue

*Age-Specific Haircare Tips*

I would be remiss if I didn't address in this book how you can polish and care for constantly evolving hair. Over the years, I've worked with people at every stage of life and learned that hair doesn't stay the same forever. What worked for your hair in your teens may fail you in your forties. The products you swore by in your twenties might leave your hair lifeless in your fifties. That's because hair, like our skin and bodies, changes with age, hormones, and lifestyle. Keeping hair healthy, full, and vibrant is possible regardless of age.

## Teenage Hair

Teen hair is often at its healthiest in terms of strength and growth rate, but that doesn't mean it's always easy to manage. Thanks to raging hormones, the scalp tends to produce more oil during adolescence, leading to greasy roots, breakouts along the hairline, and the constant need to wash. Many teens also experiment with heat tools, chemical treatments, and bold colors, often without considering the long-term damage.

What your hair needs:

- A balanced cleansing routine—washing too often can dry out the scalp, while not washing enough can cause oil buildup. A gentle, sulfate-free shampoo can help maintain a healthy balance.

- Heat protection! Whether straightening, curling, or blow-drying, protecting your hair from damage early makes all the difference later.
- A lesson in deep conditioning—hydrating masks and leave-in conditioners aren't just for dry hair; they help maintain elasticity and shine, especially if you're coloring or bleaching.

## Your Twenties and Thirties

This is the prime of your hair's life. Most people experience their thickest, fullest strands during their twenties, though lifestyle factors like diet, stress, and overprocessing can start taking a toll. By the late twenties or early thirties, you may notice subtle changes—slower growth, drier strands, or even the first grays.

What your hair needs:

- Regular trims to prevent split ends and keep hair looking fresh.
- Scalp care becomes crucial—healthy hair starts at the root, so using a scalp scrub or a lightweight oil massage can boost circulation and encourage growth.
- If coloring, opt for high-quality dyes and conditioning treatments to maintain strength.

## Your Forties and Fifties

By the forties, you start noticing real changes in your hair. Hormonal shifts—whether due to pregnancy, postpartum, or perimenopause—can lead to thinning, dryness, and changes in texture. Hair that was once straight may develop a wave, or curls might loosen. The scalp may produce less oil, leading to a drier feel overall.

If you've been coloring your hair for years, this is often when traditional dyes start to behave differently—grays become more resistant, and color might not hold as well.

**What your hair needs:**

- More moisture! A hydrating shampoo and conditioner, along with deep-conditioning treatments, help maintain elasticity.
- A gentler approach to coloring—ammonia-free dyes, glosses, or even embracing natural grays can prevent excessive damage.
- Strengthening treatments—keratin-infused masks or bond-repair treatments can help combat fragility.

### Your Sixties and Beyond

By this stage, your hair has likely changed significantly. It may be finer, drier, or even sparser in some areas. The natural graying process can also cause a shift in texture, making hair coarser or more brittle. You may choose to embrace your natural gray or continue coloring. Keeping your hair healthy is all about gentle care and nourishment.

**What your hair needs:**

- A silk or satin pillowcase to reduce friction and prevent breakage.
- A lightweight oil or serum to add shine and hydration to gray or white hair, which can sometimes appear dull.

- If thinning is a concern, a volumizing cut or a consultation with a trichologist can help explore solutions like scalp treatments or supplements.

The biggest mistake people make is sticking to the same hair routine for decades, even when their hair has changed. Just like skincare, haircare needs to evolve with age. What worked at twenty-five might not cut it at fifty. By understanding your hair's needs at each stage, you can adapt your routine, embrace changes, and ensure your hair looks and feels its best. No matter what chapter of life you're in, you can continue to polish and shine.

# ACKNOWLEDGMENTS

Thank you to my son and daughter—you are the heart of everything I do. From the moment you were born, my life took on a deeper meaning, and every step I've taken since has been with you in mind. You've seen me grow, stumble, rebuild, and rise again, and through every chapter, your love has grounded me. Being your dad is the greatest role I'll ever have, and I hope this book serves as a reminder that it's never too late to become who you truly are—that true strength comes from embracing every part of your story.

Thank you to Katie, the mother of our children, for showing me what unconditional love truly looks like. Your grace, resilience, and compassion have shaped our children in the most beautiful way. I'll always be grateful for the family we created together and the foundation of love we continue to share.

Thank you to my mum for being my first believer. You were the first to sit in my chair, the first to tell me I had something special, and the first to make me feel truly seen. Your unwavering support and love are etched into everything I do, and I carry your faith in me with deep gratitude.

Thank you to my dad. You taught me the value of hard work, humility, and staying true to myself. You didn't always have the words, but your actions spoke volumes. Your strength, steady presence, and unspoken belief in me gave me the courage to chase a life far bigger than where I started. I carry your resilience and work ethic with me every step of the way.

Thank you to my family for standing beside me through every twist and turn, reinvention and setback. Your support carried me when I didn't have the strength to keep going on my own, and your belief in me has meant more than words can express.

Thank you to Dash. You're a blue-eyed, four-legged legend with the loyalty of a lion and the attitude of a runway model. Your quiet strength, calming presence, and unconditional love have grounded me more than you'll ever know. You are truly man's best friend.

Thank you to Natasha Adamo. You came into my life like a light in the darkest of times—a one-in-a-million coach, editor, and friend who reminded me who I was when I had forgotten. You changed my life simply by being in it. There would be no book—nothing—without you.

Thank you to Amiira Ruotola and Greg Behrendt, my collaborators, writing partners, and dear friends. You helped shape this book's humor, heart, and honesty, and your creative fingerprints are everywhere in these pages. I am in eternal debt for your wisdom, generosity, and fierce friendship.

Thank you to Mariam Rastegar, my manager and friend, whose loyalty and instinct have guided me through every step of this process. Your clarity, consistency, and fierce belief in what's possible have grounded me more than you know. I'm endlessly grateful for your leadership and partnership.

Thank you to Kelly Karczewski and Dan Milaschewski at UTA for believing in this project from the very beginning and helping to shepherd it into the hands of the reader. Your advocacy and support made this journey possible.

Thank you to Grace Towery, Heather Connor, Abigail Sokolsky, and the entire team at HarperCollins for being incredible partners and true dream collaborators. Your vision, care, and attention to every detail brought this book to life in ways I never imagined. It has been an honor to create this with you.

Thank you to Clarke Crawford—truly the kind of agent you hope to find once in a lifetime. Your honesty, loyalty, and unwavering faith in my vision have meant everything. Knowing you're in my corner has made all the difference.

Thank you to Melissa Palmieri, my publicist and soul sister. You've been more than a teammate—you've been a true partner. Your passion, integrity, and refusal to settle have pushed me to think bigger and bolder. I'm so lucky to have you on this ride.

Thank you to Kim Livingston, Gail Federici, Britt Smith, and Alex Smith at Color Wow for believing in me and welcoming me like family. Collaborating with you has been one of the great joys of my career. Your trust, creative freedom, and deep support have made me feel seen, valued, and empowered in ways that are rare and unforgettable.

Thank you to Kim Kardashian. I'm honored to call you a friend. Your unwavering loyalty, resilience, and grace have inspired me for years. You are a muse in every sense of the word—a once-in-a-lifetime force. Thank you for your constant support and for showing the world that strength and softness can coexist.

To Kris Jenner, it's my honor to call you a friend, a mentor, and an inspiration. Your brilliance as a businesswoman, your strength as a mother, and your ageless grace continue to set the standard. You lead with power, purpose, and style—and remind us all that there's no limit to what a woman can accomplish at any stage of life. Thank you for showing us what's possible.

Thank you to Jennifer Lopez for being not only a friend but a guiding light throughout my career. Your generosity, wisdom, and belief in me have opened doors I never imagined. I'm endlessly grateful for the example you've set and the role you've played in my journey.

Thank you to Drew Barrymore for your heartfelt encouragement and unwavering support. Your authenticity and kindness shine through in everything you do, and your belief in me has had a lasting impact I will never forget.

To Bethenny Frankel, you're a hot, sharp-tongued hurricane in heels with the brain of a CEO and the loyalty of a wolf. Your no-bullshit brilliance, fierce friendship, and unapologetic drive to lift others up are iconic.

Thank you to Jackie Combs for being such an incredible advocate and guide throughout one of the most challenging transitions of my life. Your compassion, clarity, and dedication made all the difference. I'm deeply grateful for the support and humanity you brought to every step of this journey.

Thank you to Marty Singer. You are a true powerhouse and protector. Your unwavering integrity, sharp legal mind, and fearless advocacy have not only set the standard but made an unforgettable difference. I'm endlessly grateful for your guidance, strength, and loyalty through it all. There's no one better to have in your corner.

Thank you to Sharon Deakes. You were the one teacher who saw beyond the challenges and recognized my potential. You were the first to tell my parents not to worry; that no matter what I did in life, I'd be okay. That belief gave me a sense of safety I'd never felt before, and it changed everything. I'll always be grateful for the way you saw me when I couldn't yet see myself.

This book was born out of love, trust, and the steady presence of the people who helped me remember that I've always been enough—just as I am. Thank you for being part of this story.